Making Money with Baseball Cards

A Handbook of Insider Secrets and Strategies

Paul M. Green and Donn Pearlman

To Terry,

One of the all-Stars in
the World Series of
Collecting!

Best wishes,
Donn Pearlman

Bonus Books, Inc., Chicago

93   92   5   4

Library of Congress Catalog Card Number: 88-63236

International Standard Book Number: 0-933893-77-9

Bonus Books, Inc.
160 East Illinois Street
Chicago, Illinois 60611

Text and cover photos: James A. Simek

Printed in the United States of America

CONTENTS

ACKNOWLEDGMENTS

In addition to all those specifically mentioned by name in this book, we want to give special thanks to Bob Lemke at Krause Publications for his help over the years and his generous assistance in this effort.

Gentleman Jim Simek, a coin collecting buddy, again displayed his superb talents with a camera and a few dozen rolls of film.

Bill Deane, Senior Research Associate at the National Baseball Hall of Fame and Museum in Cooperstown, New York, always provided quick replies to our inquiries about players.

The nice folks at Bonus Books put us on the line-up for another baseball card book.

And, a big thanks for the hospitality of Chris Carson, Jr., and Jeff Morris at Carson's, the Place for Ribs, on Wells Street where a Chicago sports fan either can celebrate, or more likely, forget about that day's game.

Paul M. Green
Donn Pearlman
February 1989

Introduction

Read this even if you normally skip the Introduction chapters of other books.

Although the title of this book is *Making Money with Baseball Cards*, it could have been accurately called *How to Avoid Losing Money with Baseball Cards*. This is not just a "how to" book, it also is a "don't do" book. That may sound rather pessimistic, but we're talking about money here. Your money. And, you probably don't like losing any of it. Unfortunately, many serious investors and even casual buyers of cards currently are in the process of losing some of their cash while believing they are making only smart purchases or sales of their collections.

Just as baseball is a game, baseball card investing is, too. But it's a game where the rules keep changing.

The findings of our research, the candid comments and suggestions of the experts we've interviewed, and our own experiences in the "hobby" probably will burst quite a few bubbles of chewing gum card collectors. That's good. Unchallenged myths, misleading or outdated information, and outright falsehoods are not good for a pleasurable hobby, let alone a competitive industry that is generating up to one billion dollars a year in sales.

Before we go on to happier thoughts, ask yourself a frank question: Why would anyone *invest* in baseball cards? They're kids' stuff—pieces of colorful cardboard that should be repeatedly and delightfully traded among eager collectors until they've been fondled to death. Investments? These are not shares of IBM stock, certificates of deposit with guaranteed rates of return, or a commodities exchange contract to buy a freight train carload of corn at a future date; these are baseball cards. Why would anyone not sitting in the left field bleachers through a hot August doubleheader think there is serious money to be made with them?

The answer is twofold. First, many people truly enjoy assembling a historic collection of scarce, high-quality cards. Cards are collected for the sheer pride of ownership just as people collect beautiful rare coins, postage stamps, and works of fine art. Over a long period of time, these items generally go up in value. But perhaps more important for this book, baseball cards indeed have become a form of astoundingly profitable investment because of the greed factor.

Speculation, sudden heavy demand for specific items, and other marketplace factors can increase the values of even "common" cards quicker than Nolan Ryan's fastball moves across the plate. These price changes and the tremendous recent growth of the card collecting hobby have amazed and bewildered both beginners and advanced collectors. *Newsweek* magazine, the *New York Times*, and *Money* magazine recently have printed stories about the fabulous growth of card collecting and the huge price increases of many cards since 1980. Unfortunately, too many people apparently believe that card prices can only go up. This book emphasizes that the hobby has change-ups and curves, not just grand slams. You may know your baseball cards, but do you really know the card marketplace? Why do some cards go up in value even before they are released to the public, while others either drop or fail to significantly increase in price? Even if you are knowledgeable enough to tell the difference from the upper deck between a 1934 Goudey and a 1954 Bowman, the twists and turns of the baseball card marketplace can make you feel like you've just lost a close encounter with Billy Martin.

Sure, the hobby is filled with lucrative success stories. The 1984 Fleer Update Dwight Gooden card (#U43) easily sold for as much as $120 each as the 1986 World Series approached. Collectors and speculators made fabulous profits in only a few months. But when the 1987 World Series began, some dealers were selling the Gooden "rookie" cards for less than $50—if they could find a buyer. A slump in his on-field performance, and his off-field problems with police in Florida and illegal drugs in his body, turned public opinion at least briefly against Gooden; buyers also turned away from his baseball cards. People who purchased the cards when they were first issued in late 1984 made money even with the sharp drop in value; people who bought them at $120 can only hope Gooden's revitalized right arm glistens with 20-game gold for many years, and that his nose stays clean.

This book examines the current trends of the baseball card marketplace, providing new and valuable information about what has happened, what is happening, and what may or may not take place in the future based on established patterns in the closely related rare coin and stamp marketplaces. This book could help you make money—or at least help prevent you from losing lots of it. The authors assume you already know that *collecting* baseball cards is fun, educational, and a pastime that can and should be enjoyed with your family and friends. The authors also assume you already know that *investing* in cards can be as financially dangerous as betting on the Chicago Cubs to sweep a World Series in four straight. (Or, to bet they'll even appear in any near-future World Series.)

Baseball cards have become the penny stocks of the late 20th century. There are much safer things to do with your money, but most are not anywhere near as fun as buying a baseball card. After all, how many investors do you know who carefully store their stock certificates in sturdy, transparent protective holders so they can be frequently admired without being fondled to death?

A Busy Person's History of Baseball Cards

At least skim this chapter because there may be a few things you either forgot, or didn't know in the first place. Maybe you'll find something new to collect?

You'd be surprised how many people think all baseball cards today are packaged with bubble gum, or that cards and gum *always* came together. And many of the collectors who *do know* that not all cards are accompanied by gum, *don't know* much else about the history of cards. At least not cards issued before the last five to 30 years. If they haven't seen a particular player in action on the field, or on television, or if the retired player is not making the rounds at autograph sessions, some collectors won't bother with his cards. That's a mistake.

Dozens of different major types of cards have been issued during the last century. And among those dozens of diverse sets and series you probably will find more than 100,000 different cards. Some are very cheap despite their general rarity. We believe that when collectors become more sophisticated about the hobby they will appreciate the significance of the earlier cards, and realize how overlooked they've been in the marketplace. That will mean more demand for these cards—and higher values for them, too.

As publisher and noted collector Bob Lemke points out in the *Sports Collectors Digest Baseball Card Price Guide*, it would be impossible to list every baseball card produced in the past century, even in the price guide's 600-plus pages. However, certain card issues frequently appear in the marketplace and are actively bought and sold, some more actively than others. The following pages of this chapter contain an illustrated guide and refresher course on these major card types.

The comments here are brief. Even if you're a busy person and a long-time collector, we hope you don't skip this chapter; the information is important to know for later chapters, and besides, we've included photos of some interesting cards. More important, however, is that we believe the profit-making potential of some of these sets and individual cards is being overlooked.

For detailed information and commentary about the history of cards we recommend *The Complete Book of Collectible Baseball Cards* by the editors of Consumer Guide (written by Robert Lemke) published by Beekman House, New York, and the *Sports Collectors Digest Baseball Card Encyclopedia*, from Krause Publications. Other strongly recommended books and hobby publications are listed in chapter 14.

Now, if you are among those who either think all cards today come with chewing gum, or that gum and cards were *always* synonymous, you are about to have your first bubble burst.

SMOKE GETS IN YOUR EYES – CARDS GET IN YOUR HANDS

Fierce competition among tobacco companies produced the first major sets of baseball cards. In the late 1880s, small cards measuring only about 1-1/2 by 2-1/2 inches were included with packages of cigarettes as promotional items. (The relationship between cards and bubble gum was still a few years away.) While some very rare earlier cards are known, their origins are still obscure.

The era of the "tobacco cards" apparently began in the mid-1880s with the Richmond, Virginia, tobacco company, Allen & Ginter, using cards to increase sales. But the first major promotion of a card set was launched in 1886 by the New York-based Goodwin & Company's "Old Judge" brand of cigarettes. Woodcut drawings of baseball players appeared on the front of the cards

Typical of the "action" shots that actually were posed in a photographer's studio, this 1887-1890 era card of player Harry Stovey is from the Old Judge set cataloged as N-172.

with advertising for the cigarettes on the back. Researchers believe these first cards apparently were distributed only in the New York city area. The evidence is rather strong: All of the 11 players pictured on these cards were members of the New York National League team.

The baseball card idea started by John Allen and Major Lewis Ginter was imitated quickly. In 1887 there were a half dozen cigarette brands issuing cards with their tobacco products. Some of the names are very colorful, Buchner Gold Coin, Kalamazoo Bats, and Lone Jack. Some brands used sepia-toned photographs, others began using multi-color lithographs. Some card backs were blank, some contained advertising, some carried checklists so collectors could keep track of what cards they still needed to complete their sets.

Allen & Ginter produced a set of "World Champion" cards, ten of the cards honored baseball players including six eventual members of the Hall of Fame. The Goodwin & Company cards of 1887 featured players in posed photographs which by today's stan-

Hall of Famer Charles Comiskey is one of six HOFers depicted in the Allen & Ginter tobacco cards set of 1887.

dards seem quaint at best and comical at worst. Close examination of these "action" shots clearly shows they were made inside the photographer's studio, a string holding the baseball "hurling toward" the fielder's glove and a fluffy carpet of "grass" supporting the base to which a player has just safely "slid."

For collectors, though, there is nothing funny about the fact that 117 players of the era are depicted in a wide assortment of these poses, and baseball card collecting was becoming a hobby. All cards considered, 1887 is perhaps the most significant year for the early baseball card historian, and a fascinating year for the baseball card collector. The Goodwin "Old Judge" cards are excellent as a specialized collection, while the Allen & Ginter cards capture the spirit of baseball before the turn of the century in a way that is hard to describe.

By 1888 you practically needed a checklist just to keep track of all the different cigarette brands giving away baseball cards. In addition to six tobacco companies, The G & B Company of New York included cards with its nationally distributed chewing gum.

There would not be another major issue of gum and cards together until 1933, although other confectionary companies started using cards as promotional items around the turn of the century.

The first big relationship between cards and candies occurred in 1908 when the American Caramel Company of Philadelphia put baseball cards in packages of caramel candy. But not all the names on the cards actually matched the players depicted on them during the three years the sets were issued. (This strange practice also is found on other early card sets.) Researchers believe only 33 players' pictures were used for 75 different ballplayers' names in the 1908 American Caramel Company sets. But unless the caramel-chewing collectors got two cards with different names but the same picture, they probably wouldn't know the difference. Remember, fans in those days didn't see their super stars on television or have the luxury of scanning their choice of dozens of glossy, color-photo-filled sports magazines, although there were popular sports journals of the day.

Between 1909 and 1911, American Caramel produced a much better quality set called "Base Ball Caramels" and designated by collectors as series E-90-1. (Researcher Jeff Burdick came up with the letter and number combination to designate baseball card series in his book, *The American Card Catalog*.) These actually had the correct players matched with their names, although usually only the player's last name was printed on the card. This series bears a rather close resemblance to the famous T-206 series of tobacco cards. The backside reads, "BASE BALL SERIES/100 SUBJECTS/BASE BALL CARAMELS/MFG' BY/ AMERICAN CARAMEL CO./PHILA., PA." Despite the claim, "100 subjects," about 120 major variations are known.

Just as the tobacco companies began quickly copying the card concept from each other, caramel and other candy makers also distributed several dozen different sets between 1910 and 1920. Many of the manufacturers used the same color lithographs of the players for the fronts of their cards and just changed advertising slogans, logos, and wording on the backs to promote their own products.

The Collins-McCarthy Candy Company of San Francisco became very active in cards during this time. Among other products, they produced a caramel-coated popcorn candy called Zee Nut (or

Two of the sixteen different brands of cigarettes advertised on the backs of T-206 series baseball cards, Sweet Caporal and Piedmont.

Zeenut), and for 28 years beginning in 1911 they gave away cards with their Zeenut, Ruf-Neks, and Home Run Kisses candy products. Most of the players were from the Pacific Coast League. In 1916, the company distributed a 200 card black and white photo set called "BASEBALL'S HALL of FAME." That title is a bit deceptive. Many of the players in the E-135 set may have visited Cooperstown by bus, but they are not enshrined there.

The big era of tobacco cards centers on the years 1909 to 1915. It was during this time that the famous T-206 series was produced. Issued between 1909 and 1911, the T-206 series has been estimated as having more than 7,500 possible combinations of players on the front and advertising for 16 different cigarette brands on the back. That's why most collectors just try to assemble a set based only on who is depicted on the front of the cards. The authoritative *Sports Collectors Digest Baseball Card Price Guide* lists 524 cards in a "complete" set, including such variations as the player's pose and/or his team affiliation.

The T-206 usually is referred to as the "white borders" to-

The "King of Cards," the famous and expensive T-206 Honus Wagner. Wagner was one of the five original inductees in the Baseball Hall of Fame in 1936 along with Ty Cobb, Walter Johnson, Christy Mathewson, and Babe Ruth.

An ornate border design highlights the Roy Hartzell card from the Ramly Cigarettes series (T-209) of 1909.

HOFer Walter Johnson is shown on this example of a T-205 series gold border card.

bacco cards because the color lithograph pictures of the players are surrounded by white borders (a rare example of logic in the card collecting hobby). The T-206 white border cards are the most popular of the tobacco sets because of their colorful appearance and their general availability. Some notably rare cards in the set include the so-called "King of Cards," featuring Honus Wagner, the Hall of Fame Pittsburgh shortstop. A superb example of the T-206 Wagner reportedly changed hands for more than $100,000 in early 1988, shattering all previous records for that or any other baseball card. (Values like that can mislead people to believe that *all* old baseball cards are worth really big money, and to falsely reason that if a card from 1911 is worth $100,000 then surely a card from 1909 is worth even more because it is older.)

In 1911, a similar-sized set of small cards was issued with gold borders framing the players. Logically, this series has been given the hobby name, "gold borders." Not so logically, even though this series actually was issued *after* the T-206 cards, it has been numbered T-205. You figure it out, we can't. But then we still can't figure out why Atlanta, located in the Southeastern part of the United States, is listed in the National League's Western Division.

In addition to the cigarette advertising on the back, the T-205 cards of major league players carry a short biography and some statistical information. The dozen minor leaguers contained in the set have no stats on the backs of their cards.

Other tobacco cards from the era include the T-204 Ramly Turkish Cigarettes and T.T.T. brand cards issued in 1909 with black and white photos and very decorative borders. These are rather scarce and their already high prices tend to limit their collectibility. Three sets of baseball cards picturing players from the Pacific Coast and Northwest Leagues were distributed in the Western United States between 1909 and 1911 with Obak brand cigarettes, a subsidiary of American Tobacco Company which was responsible for the T-206 series. Two other significant regional sets were issued between 1909 and 1910 in the Mid-Atlantic area states by Contentnea brand cigarettes featuring players from the Carolina Association, and the Virginia and Eastern Carolina Leagues. One small set has color drawings of the players, the other, larger set of about 200 cards has black and white photographs.

The Turkey Red brand cigarette cards of 1911 are rather high-

Almost as big as a breadbox! A 25 cent piece is dwarfed by the size of this 1911 John Franklin "Home Run" Baker cabinet card from Turkey Red Cigarettes (T-3).

priced, but their larger size (8 by 5-3/4 inch) has earned them the nickname "cabinet cards" and generated an admiring following of collectors. The two most expensive "Turkey Reds" T-3 series cards are those of Hall of Fame players Ty Cobb and Walter Johnson. The series is called "Prominent Base Ball Players & Athletes," and about two dozen boxers are depicted along with 100 baseball players on the different cards. In addition to ads for Turkey Red cigarettes, the cards may also carry ads for Fez and Old Mill brands. Smaller-sized Old Mill cards also were distributed in the Southeastern United States in 1910. Much more research is needed on this card issue logically known as "Red Borders" because of the distinctive color of the front borders. It includes more than 600 known different cards with players of eight different baseball leagues and associations. One of the Blue Grass League cards features a youngster named Casey Stengel who would be inducted into the Hall of Fame in 1966 for his achievements in baseball management, not as a player.

The New Orleans-based Red Sun cigarette company, also

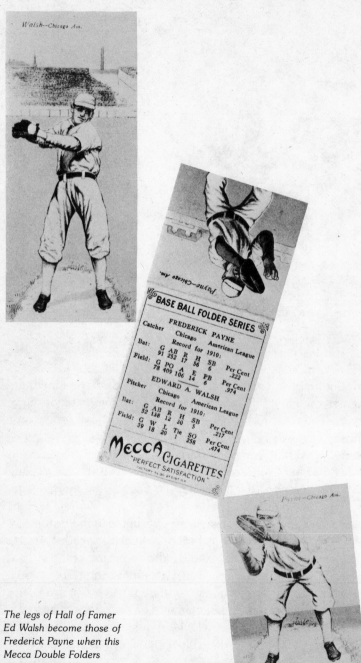

The legs of Hall of Famer
Ed Walsh become those of
Frederick Payne when this
Mecca Double Folders
(T-201) card of 1911 is
folded.

part of American Tobacco Company, produced black and white photo cards. This Southeast regional set of 75 cards features Southern Association players.

In 1911 the Mecca Cigarette Company introduced what we now call "Mecca double folders." These cards were designed to be doubled up and folded. If you hold the card one way, you see a drawing of one player; but when you fold it properly, a second player appears with his upper body now using the lower torso portion of the first player. In this T-201 set there are 50 different cards with a total of 100 different players; but only 50 pairs of legs. The cards also carried statistical information on the players. Because the cards were intended to be folded and creased, it is extremely rare to find a truly mint example.

Interestingly, what we take for granted today—the biographical and statistical data on a card—really didn't appear to any great extent until nearly three decades after the first major baseball cards were issued.

Borrowing from both the T-201 Mecca double folders and the T-205 gold border sets, the Hassan Cigarette brand issued a 132 card set (including major variations) that carried three pictures—two were player portraits and the third was an "action" drawing between them—and they all were surrounded by a gold border. The "Mecca triple folders" also contain biographical information about the players, and most specimens today have (at least) two creases.

In 1912, a set of cards similar to the T-205 and T-206 cards was produced. Similar, but still different enough to be rejected by many collectors today. The T-207 cards just don't have enough eye appeal, an increasingly important factor in the desirability of cards. The T-207s have tan borders surrounding sepia and white drawings of 200 different players. The backgrounds of the pictures are brown. "Dull" is the word used most often to describe this otherwise historic set.

Also of note from this era are the T-200s, the Ligget & Myers Tobacco Company 1913 Fatima brand cigarette cards picturing team photographs of the 16 ballclubs that comprised the American and National Leagues. If you saved the special coupons from 40 packages of Fatima cigarettes you could obtain a 21 by 13 inch enlargement of the team card. Both the smaller (4-3/4 by 2-5/8 inch) and larger cards are known as "Fatima team cards," however, the larger cards are much rarer than the smaller ones.

Pittsburgh star Honus Wagner, who reportedly demanded that his T-206 card be removed from distribution because he did not advocate cigarette smoking, can be found as one of the players in two color drawings on the tobacco cards regionally distributed in 1914 and 1915 by the Peoples Tobacco Company of New Orleans.

Anyone who seriously wants to collect tobacco cards must own a copy of researcher/dealer Lew Lipset's impressive books, *The Encyclopedia of Baseball Cards*. You'll find details about this three-volume book in chapter 14.

It only seems natural that eventually some company whose business actually involved sports would get involved in the baseball card craze that was building after the turn of the century. The weekly *Sporting Life* newspaper (not to be confused with *The Sporting News* which issued its own cards) started printing coupons in its pages in 1911 that were good for a free card. In all, there are 24 different sets with a combined total of 288 cards in the *Sporting Life* series, each card resembling the famous T-206 white borders but with advertising for the weekly Saturday five cent newspaper on the back.

The Sporting News joined its sports media competition with a card offering in 1916. Two different but very similar sets were offered by mail to readers, and the black and white photographs are the same ones that already did or were soon to appear on the cards of various caramel companies.

Starting in 1921, the Exhibit Supply Co. of Chicago produced a series of large baseball cards, each the size of a picture postcard. These usually were sold for a penny each in vending machines. The last "Exhibits" were issued in 1963.

CARDS & CONFECTION–THE START OF GUM & CARAMEL STAINS

The American Caramel Company which, as we mentioned earlier, began issuing baseball cards in 1908 was a major player during the Roaring '20s. They came to bat in 1921 with two very similar-appearing sets, both labeled E-121 today. Although the backs of their 1921 cards claim "This set consists of pictures of eighty of the leading BASE BALL STARS of the AMERICAN AND NATIONAL LEAGUES," more than 120 different kinds of cards with black and white photos actually were distributed. The similar-appearing set, distributed by American Caramel in 1922,

A typical 1910 era
candy/caramel card of
HOFer Christy Mathewson,
misspelled on this example
from the E-102 series.

indicates there are 120 leading stars in the series; however, collectors have discovered there are at least 125 different kinds of cards.

Perhaps the most popular set American Caramel issued is E-120, a series of 240 cards that accompanied sticks of caramel candy in 1922. The cards showing American League players have brown ink on a yellow background; those with National League players are green against blue-green. Even though the printer made a spelling mistake, the Ty "Cob" card is one of the prizes in this set.

One of the most impressive-looking card sets was produced by the Cracker Jack Company and distributed in boxes of their still popular caramel-coated popcorn treat. The 1914 set, E-145-1, contains the stars of the day from the Federal as well as American and National Leagues. There are 144 cards in the 1914 set, and 176 in the 1915 series, E-145-2. Even though the front of the cards may look exactly the same it is easy to tell the two series apart. The back side of the 1914 series proclaims "Complete set has 144 pictures. . . ," while the 1915 cards do not carry that number.

One of the problems in determining rarity of most baseball cards is the lack of information about how many cards originally were printed or actually distributed. The modern card companies claim the data are proprietary information and they keep their seven, eight, and nine digits production numbers a trade secret.

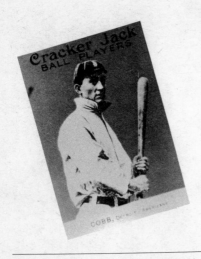

From 1914, a Cracker Jack card showing HOFer Ty Cobb.

Back in 1914, Cracker Jack was proud to proclaim it intended to print 10 million cards. By the time the higher-numbered cards were being issued later in the year, that figure had jumped to 15 million. Despite the large quantity, superb quality specimens are scarce because the cards were printed on heavy paper, but not cardboard, and therefore, were very easily bent, folded, and otherwise mutilated. Most Cracker Jack cards also have stain marks on one or both sides of the cards from contact with the Cracker Jack candy. Unstained, superb quality specimens are rare.

Still, their impressive appearance, the tinted red background photographs of Hall of Fame players, and the biographical information about those stars on the backs, make the Cracker Jack players among the most desired of all E-series cards. These pre-World War I cards are never confused with the 16 card set produced by Topps for Cracker Jack in 1982.

The U.S. Caramel Company of East Boston, Massachusetts, issued the last major caramel card sets of the era in 1932, a series of black and white photos with red backgrounds and white borders with each card showing one of 31 "famous athletes" including 26 baseball players. The cards measure 2-1/2 by 3 inches and at first glance look similar to the Cracker Jack issues of 1914 and 1915. Ty Cobb, Lou Gehrig, and Babe Ruth are among the players in this often overlooked and scarce series.

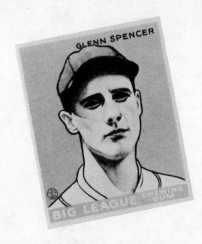

*New York Giants player
Glenn Spencer is on this
1933 Goudey card. The
not-quite-truthful claim on
the back, "This is one of a
series of 240 Baseball
Stars."*

The 1933 set distributed by Goudey Gum Company of Boston is considered by most collectors to be the first of the modern
era of bubble gum baseball cards. As mentioned earlier, some
cards were distributed with gum in 1888, but the association of
baseball cards and candy products did not develop until nearly two
decades later. The relationship between cards used as a premium
to sell chewing gum really blossomed during the Depression years
of the 1930s. Well, we've come full circle. Now the gum is the premium included with some cards.

In 1933, Goudey sold a stick of gum with one baseball card
for just one cent. All those cards certainly are worth considerably
more than a penny apiece today. Each card contains a color drawing of a player's portrait or the player in action on the field, and biographical information is printed on the backside. Goudey issued
cards in 1933, '34, '35, '36, '38, and 1941. Each set is distinctive,
although some sets are much more popular than others.

The 1933 Goudey is a classic for two big reasons. First, it was
the beginning of the modern era of the gum cards (and marked a
decade-long drought of major new baseball cards), and second,
the set is loaded with super stars of the era whose names are still
familiar today: Babe Ruth is on four cards in the set and there are
cards of Lou Gehrig, Jimmy Foxx, Rogers Hornsby, Dizzy Dean,
and Lefty Grove, among others. A complete set has 240 cards, but

that is misleading. The Goudey Gum Company, in a scheme that would make almost any marketing executive smile with envy, declared on the back of each card, "This is one of a series of 240 Baseball Stars." But the company apparently only produced 239 different cards. This trick kept youngsters shelling out lots of pennies trying to obtain the elusive, missing 240th card (#106) to complete their sets. Some irate customers wrote to Goudey complaining about the unavailable card. Goudey eventually printed a #106 card depicting Napoleon (Larry) Lajoie, a slugger with a lifetime batting average of .339, but whose 21 year career actually had ended nearly two decades earlier. These Lajoie cards are quite scarce, valued at several thousand dollars even in dog-eared condition.

The 1933 Goudey set has been given the American Card Catalog designation, R-319, but everyone calls it "'33 Goudeys." "Sport Kings" is another 1933 set issued by Goudey, but only three baseball players are pictured in the 48 card set of well known football, hockey, basketball players and even wrestlers. This set also looks very different from the regular 1933 Goudey Baseball Stars cards.

The 1934 Goudey set contains 96 cards and a quote from either Lou Gehrig or Chuck Klein in addition to the color drawing and biographical information on those two players or other major leaguers of the day. The 1935 Goudey cards are multiple player cards, each of the 36 different cards has the drawings of four players on the front, so they usually are referred to as "four-in-ones." The backside of each card has a piece of a puzzle, and the nine completed puzzles compose the portraits of different players or team photographs.

The 1936 Goudey set is only 25 cards with black and white photographs of individual players on the front and brief biographical data on the back. The back also is printed with various designations such as "FOUL/Over the press boxes.," or "BALL/Too high and wide." Young collectors of 1936 could shuffle their stacks of baseball cards and deal them out to play a game of "baseball." These cards are rather scarce today in top condition compared to other Goudey issues, apparently for two reasons. First, they were not all that popular when they were first issued, and second, many youngsters who did purchase them played with the cards because

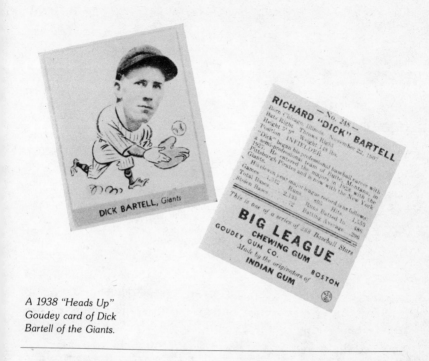

A 1938 "Heads Up"
Goudey card of Dick
Bartell of the Giants.

of the baseball game printed on the back. Due to the frequent handling, many of the cards were not carefully preserved. Even with
general scarcity of high grade specimens, they don't attract too
many collectors now because the black and white photos of the
players lack eye appeal, that vital element of desirability.

Perhaps the second most popular Goudey set, behind the famous 1933 issue, is the 1938 "Heads Up" set. The series consists
of 48 cards, even though the backs of the cards indicate "This is
one of a series of 288 Baseball Stars," and each card has a photograph of the head of a player with the rest of his body drawn as a
cartoon. These cards were not overwhelmingly popular with collectors for many years, but the trend seems to be turning in favor of
the Heads Up set. A third of the players pictured in the set now are
in the Hall of Fame and these are the first major baseball cards of
Bob Feller and Joe DiMaggio.

Goudey's last card set was issued in 1941, a not very attractive
series of 33 players shown in black and white photos with a single
color for the background and the company's brand name, "Big

A Boston sportswriter's comments appear on the back of this 1934-1936 era Diamond Stars series card showing Ted Lyons of the Chicago White Sox.

League Gum," with a baseball logo in a corner. Nothing is printed on the backs of the cards. Collectors seem to shun these cards. Maybe they're right, but this was the last set of the company that launched the golden age of baseball cards and chewing gum.

Most of the attention on cards of the 1930s is focused on the Goudeys, yet there are a half dozen other significant bubblegum issues of the period. Chicago-based Orbit Gum Company placed one card in each one cent pack of its Tattoo brand gum. The black and white photo is over a color drawing of a ballpark, while the backsides do not contain stats and only very brief biographical information. There are 60 different cards in the Tattoo Orbit set. The DeLong Gum Company of Boston issued its first and only card set in 1933, an interesting series of black and white photos of players superimposed over a color drawing of a ballpark. DeLong's product was called "Play Ball," and while this name appears on the backs of the 1933 DeLong set, it should not be confused with another "Play Ball" card set issued six years later by the Gum Company of Philadelphia.

Another Massachusetts chewing gum maker, National Chicle Gum Company of Cambridge, launched two different series of cards in 1934, "Batter Up" and "Diamond Stars." Both series were produced for three years. The Batter Up set is 192 black and white or color tinted full-figure photos that were die cut, intended to be

One of the least expensive major cards of "Shoeless" Joe Jackson is from the 1940 Play Ball set.

punched out so the player appears to be standing up. Cards that have not been folded are worth considerably more than cards that have been played with. The Diamond Stars cards, printed on thick cardboard, are composed of 108 color drawings of the players on the front and baseball tips written by Boston newspaper writers on the back. A complete set of different front and back combinations totals 168 cards, but most collectors just assemble sets by considering the front side, not what's on the back.

The Play Ball series launched in 1939 by Gum, Inc., marked a big improvement in the previous quality of black and white photos on cards. The series also set a precedent in providing more extensive biographical information about the players. The Ted Williams rookie card (#92) is found in this popular 162 card set.

The 1940 Play Ball cards are significantly different from the 1939 set. The player's photo on the front has a "frame" around it, and some of those players, like "Twinkletoes" Selkirk and "Poosh 'Em Up Tony" Lazzeri, and their unusual nicknames had never before appeared on any other baseball cards. One of the least expensive cards available of "Shoeless Joe" Jackson (#225) is in this 240 card set. (Banned for life from the game of baseball because of the 1919 "Black Sox" scandal, Jackson's lifetime batting average was .356 and his quick work playing left field earned his glove the appropriate title, "The place triples go to die."

HOFer Yogi Berra's rookie card (#6) is in the 1948 debut series from Bowman. More information about this card is in chapter 7.

The 1941 Play Ball cards have color toned photos of players. Only 72 different cards were issued in this series, but one of them is the rookie card (#54) of Harold "Pee Wee" Reese, the Hall of Fame Brooklyn Dodgers shortstop.

WORLD WAR II ENDS—THE CARD WARS BEGIN

The need for paper and rubber products during World War II halted the manufacturing of baseball cards, but soon after the war ended a new era of cards began. More than a dozen regional issues were produced in 1946 and 1947, including cards produced for Sunbeam brand bread and the Remar Baking Company that featured Pacific Coast League players, and Tip Top Bread with players from major league teams in the Northeast and Midwest.

The post World War II baseball card era gained momentum in 1948 when the Bowman chewing gum company of Philadelphia and the Leaf confectionary company of Chicago issued their first sets. Although the Bowman 48 card set has black and white photography—a drawback to some collectors—about a fourth of the set consists of Hall of Fame players such as Bob Feller, Stan Musial, and Warren Spahn. This is the first set issued by Bowman, a major name in card collecting of the early 1950s. The Leaf set only has 98 different cards, but the numbering system spread out between late 1948 and into 1949 goes to number 168, apparently

"The Old Professor," HOFer Casey Stengel (#217) as shown on one of the small, square cards with apparently good investment potential, the 1950 Bowman series.

a throw-back to the earlier mentioned 1933 attempt by the Goudey company which aimed to get youngsters to spend their pennies hunting for missing (and nonexistent) cards. The Leaf cards have a color-tinted black and white photo on the front and the set includes such stars as Ted Williams, Bob Feller, Satchell Paige, Joe DiMaggio, and even former players Babe Ruth and Honus Wagner.

The first Topps baseball cards also were issued in 1948, but they do not resemble typical cards. The 19 different baseball players cards produced by Topps were part of a 252 card set of "Magic Photos" that would automatically develop when exposed to sunlight. Hall of Fame players such as Honus Wagner, Ty Cobb, Lou Gehrig, Cy Young, and Walter Johnson are in the set, but the overall card quality is not very good.

The Bowman company color tinted its black and white photos for its 1949 set, a huge set for those days—240 different cards. The 1949 Bowman issue is the first large scale set produced since World War II and is filled with both super stars and many "common" players of the era who are not pictured on any other baseball cards. Among the famous rookies in the set are Duke Snider and Robin Roberts.

In 1950 Bowman retained the small size for its cards, 2-1/16 by 2-1/2 inches, but improved the graphics. Color paintings were

The rookie card of HOFer Whitey Ford is the first card in the 324 card set issued by Bowman in 1951.

used for the 252 card set that is considered a classic by many collectors. Not just players were depicted on the cards. Bowman included well-known managers of the day like Casey Stengel and Leo Durocher. (A few years later, Bowman would even put umpires on some cards.)

Bowman significantly enlarged both the size of its cards and the size of its set in 1951, going to 324 different cards, again with color paintings of the players. Rookies Whitey Ford, Willie Mays, and Mickey Mantle made their card debut on 1951 Bowmans. Biographical information fills most of the backside of the cards. Because the cards are larger, 2-1/16 by 3-1/8 inches, more people seem to collect 1951 Bowmans than the company's earlier, smaller-sized issues.

The Topps Chewing Gum Company of Brooklyn, New York, re-entered the card marketplace in 1951 with five different sets: An 11 card Current All-Stars set of die-cut cards designed to be folded so the player stands up; a similar set of 11 die-cut cards called Connie Mack All-Stars; a scarce nine card set with 5-1/4 by 2-1/16 inches photographs of nine major league teams (some cards have the date 1950 on them, others do not); and two well-known sets that were designed to be used as game pieces, the 1951 Topps "Red Backs" and "Blue Backs," so named because some have red colored backs, others are blue. These are 52 card sets with a black

OUTFIELD
NEW YORK GIANTS
Born: Westfield, Ala., May 6, '31
Height: 5-10½   Weight: 170
Bats: Right   Throws: Right
The National League's Rookie
of the Year Army-bound Willie
had appeared in 35 games for
Millers and had a .477 batting
average when Giants called him
up. Hit .274 for the Giants and
drove in 68 runs. Had 22 doubles
and 20 homers. A speed demon,
made sensational play against
Dodgers, making a catch in
deep center and throwing run-
ner out at plate

1952 RED MAN ALL-STAR TEAM
NATIONAL LEAGUE SERIES—PLAYER #15

Decades after the first, historic tobacco cards were issued, Red Man Chewing Tobacco issued its own set in 1952. This one (#15-N) shows HOFer Willie Mays.

and white player's photo on the front along with a word like "BALL" or "STRIKE" so the cards could be shuffled and a game of baseball acted out. Because of the discovery of a small hoard, the Red Backs are easier to find than the Blue Backs, but outside the hoard, the Blue Backs generally have survived in better conditon because they were printed on slightly thicker cardboard. Both sets have rounded corners.

Production of baseball cards exploded in 1952. Post World War II regional cards were churned out since 1946, but two partic-ular issues stand out in 1952: Red Man and Mother's Cookies. From 1952 through 1955, the Red Man chewing tobacco com-pany issued cards featuring current stars of the game. Each 3-1/2 by 4 inch card had a small tab across the bottom that was intended to be torn off and mailed to the company to obtain a free baseball cap. Red Man cards with the tab still attached are worth considera-bly more than those with it removed. These are historic cards—the first "tobacco cards" in four decades—but are rather inexpensive considering their comparative rarity to other issues of the era.

The Mother's Cookies Company of California started a long-running tradition of issuing baseball cards in 1952 with a 64 card set featuring Pacific Coast League players. (For more information on these cards see chapter 9.)

Topps and Bowman battled it out in 1952 and that battle continues today between collectors who claim the 1952 Topps is *the* all-time greatest set and others who believe the 1952 Bowman set is among the most appealing. Bowman used artists' paintings for the 252 cards in the 1952 set. Topps issued a huge 407 card set with hand-colored black and white photos of the players, a team logo in color, and lots of statistics with the players' biographies on the back. An entire encyclopedia could (and should) be written about the 1952 Topps and Bowman cards. It would make fascinating reading. But since this chapter already is longer than originally planned by the authors, we'll conclude by repeating that these two sets are among the most popular ever produced and prices for even common cards (let alone the 1952 Topps Mickey Mantle) reflect that popularity and demand.

Over the next three years, Topps and Bowman continued their fight to secure the rights for printing pictures of major league players and obtaining the largest possible share of the baseball card market. The cards issued since the 1950s have been and continue to be thoroughly covered by current hobby publications. We can briefly summarize here the fascinating Topps and Bowman cards of the era by simply stating they changed their designs and sometimes the card sizes each year, and Bowman issued its last set in 1955, the famous "tv set" that shows each player framed by the drawing of a color television set. Nearly three dozen umpires also are depicted on 1955 Bowman cards.

After that, Topps purchased Bowman and for the next two and a half decades it was virtually a card market monopoly for Topps. A few, limited, national card sets were produced as sales premiums, and many regional card issues were produced, of course. Kahn's Wieners, the Cincinnati meat company that started using cards as promotional items in 1955, was one such regional issue. (Buying a Kahn's Wieners hot dog is still part of the joy of attending a Reds game at Riverfront Stadium.) Some of these card issues are covered in later chapters.

Fleer Corporation of Philadelphia entered the card market in 1959 with a single theme set of 80 cards featuring the life story of slugger Ted Williams. These cards were sold with bubblegum setting the stage for a series of legal battles that would continue on and off for two decades. Who had the rights to sell baseball cards with gum or any confectionary item? When the Leaf Company is-

Former player turned umpire, Thomas Gorman (#293), is one of 31 umps featured in the last Bowman series, the famous 1955 "tv set."

sued a 1960 set of cards they included a marble in the package rather than gum! Fleer's 1960-1962 old-timers sets featuring "Baseball Greats" were issued with chewing gum, but the 1963 cards of current players were accompanied by a small cookie. The next Fleer set would not hit the marketplace until 1981.

Perhaps the most significant baseball card event of the 1970s occurred in 1974. For the first time, Topps issued its regular 660 card set all at once. Prior to 1974, lower numbered cards were distributed first, then the higher numbered cards would be released later in the season. That's why high-numbered pre-1974 cards often are much scarcer and more valuable than lower numbers. Collecting interest would drop off later in the season when it was obvious many teams would not be even close to appearing in the World Series, and the card companies usually printed smaller quantities of the higher numbered cards. In 1974 that changed and the new tradition of being able to get an entire set early in the year began. (It also started a new tradition of price gouging by some merchants who charge outrageous amounts of money for just-released cards in January and February. If over-eager collectors would wait a few months they probably can purchase those still-being printed card sets for less money in April and May. Early season scrambling to obtain the first shipments causes distribution problems and prompts some wholesalers and retailers to pump up prices. There are plenty of cards to go around. If more collectors will be patient and refuse to pay too much for current cards, prices will quickly return to their proper, early season levels. They will then increase and decrease based on the merit of the sets and the players they contain.)

Since 1981, Topps has the exclusive rights to package their baseball cards with gum, so other card issuers often use stickers, team logos, and puzzles as premiums. In that year, Fleer ended its 18-year absence from the card market by producing a 660 card set and the Donruss Company of Memphis, a division of Leaf Company, also entered the marketplace for the first time with a 600 card set. During the 1980s, many more regional and promotional issues enticed collectors and several other nationally-distributed cards made their debut, among them Star, Sportflics, and Score. The manufacturers usually produce regular sets early in the year and all sorts of various special sets as the season continues. Updated sets containing 100 to 150 cards arrive around World Series time to reflect player trades and hot rookies who may have been overlooked back in January when the regular issue sets were first released.

The high-tech Sportflics cards, first introduced in 1986 with the assistance of the Wrigley Company of Chicago, show three different pictures in one depending how light strikes the surface of the cards. The initial thrill of the new "Magic Motion" cards appears to have worn off, though, and Sportflics at this time do not appear to be a major threat to the Big Three of the card business, Donruss, Fleer and Topps. Some of the people involved in the Sportflics cards, Major League Marketing of Stamford, Connecticut, conducted extensive market research and introduced another card set in 1988, Score. Each Score card includes a *color* portrait of the player with biographical information on the back as well as an excellent color action shot on the front. The premier edition includes 660 cards, each the same size as the regular cards of the other major card manufacturers, 2-2/3 by 3-1/2 inches.

Collector reaction to Score cards so far has been very positive. Readers of *Baseball Hobby News* (BHN) ranked Score the number one set in 1988, followed by Topps, Fleer, and Donruss. The BHN survey story writer, Scott Miller, flatly stated, "The Big Three is now officially the Big Four."

New York Mets star Darryl
Strawberry in action on his
1986 Sportflics "Magic
Motion" card (#97).

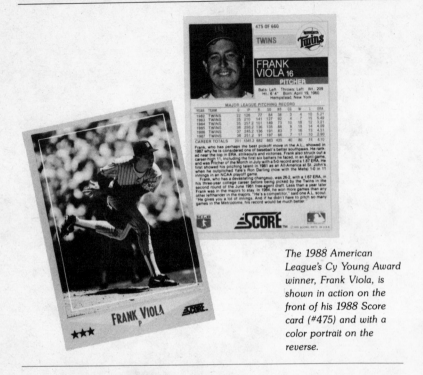

The 1988 American League's Cy Young Award winner, Frank Viola, is shown in action on the front of his 1988 Score card (#475) and with a color portrait on the reverse.

Perhaps that's a bit premature. Topps certainly is solidly commanding the major share of the market for both current as well as earlier cards and the company's management is well aware of the competition, yet collecting trends can and do change over the years. One thing is certain, there already are tens of thousands of different baseball cards to collect and the number of possible items to purchase grows by thousands each year.

The Bizarre Bazaar

The Invasion of the Coin Dealers and other tales of temerity.

Major dealers, who are involved in baseball cards literally seven days a week, have been amazed at the explosive growth of the baseball card market. No one predicted it even a few years ago.

"No, no one could have told about this market. If I knew the market (ahead of time) I'd be a genius!," laughed prominent dealer Al "Mr. Mint" Rosen of New Jersey.

Veteran California dealer Tony Galovich agrees. "I expected it to go up, but it's gone up more than I anticipated. It just keeps growing because of the influx of collectors and investors. I've been around the market for a long time and the amount of press coverage we're getting now is unprecedented and incredible, and it's virtually all positive."

A story about baseball cards by United Press International in March 1988 contained an estimate that nationwide sales of cards that year would top $250 million (with perhaps "only" $50 million of that for cards produced before 1950). The story also quoted card hobby publisher James Beckett as saying he would not be surprised to learn that perhaps $1 million had been spent just on Mickey Mantle cards in the first five months after the "Black Monday" stock market crash of Oct. 19, 1987.

By September 1988 the estimates had ballooned. *Advertising Age,* a respected, weekly marketing industry publication, quoted sources who thought baseball card sales that year perhaps could top a billion dollars ($1,000,000,000) with about $350 million of that amount in the re-sale market of older cards, the remainder being spent on current items.

As mentioned before, the major card manufacturers do not make public their production figures, but conservative estimates peg the Big Three's combined output in 1988 at more than 5,000,000,000 (five BILLION) cards. That's a conservative estimate, and it does not include other manufacturers such as Score, Star, minor league card producers, or companies that offer cards as sales premiums, such as Mother's Cookies. If investing in these items is "a house of cards," it's a very, very big house.

The general news media devoted considerable attention to baseball cards in 1988, adding lots of new fuel to the buying and selling fires. The UPI story in March was followed in April with a *New York Times* feature article in a Sunday edition, "Investors Hope a Rich Future Is in the Cards," that quoted Dr. Beckett and Frank Barning of *BHN* about the hobby-investment boom. In June, *Money Magazine* presented readers with an illustration-filled article based on the research of David S. Krause, assistant professor of finance at Marquette University in Milwaukee who combined his love of collecting with his expertise in economics and statistics to objectively measure the baseball card market from 1978 through 1987. His bottom line, according to *Sports Collectors Digest:* Baseball cards for the last ten years have risen approximately 32 percent per year. Rookie cards have risen approximately 45 percent.

To understand where baseball cards are today and where they may be headed, it's probably wise to understand something about where they've been. Countless numbers of American mothers (Hi, Mom, this means YOU!) have been indicted, tried, and convicted by outraged kids who had a fortune in baseball cards land in the local trash dump during an infamous Spring Cleaning or when the offspring was away at camp, college or wherever.

To everyone who learned about the missing collection and screamed, "Say it ain't so, Mom!," let's be fair to her. Baseball cards have been around for over 100 years, but we've considered them really valuable for only about 10. Find anyone over the age of 25 who had cards as a kid and you'll discover that 99 percent of them were card sadists. They attached them to bicycle spokes, flipped them repeatedly against plaster, wood, and brick walls, carried them around bundled with a rubber band in a back pocket, left them littered all over the house, perhaps even traded a Mantle for a favorite player of the day, like Wes Westrum (who?). So, don't blame Mom, too much.

In fairness to her, the state of the baseball card market and the hobby in the 1950s and earlier was rather simple to describe. There was none. There were no publications, weekly or monthly, with page after page of stories, pictures, and advertisements about baseball cards. There was no national convention of collectors, no 200 page price guides, no "Mr. Mint" spending more than a million dollars a year to buy cards.

Instead, decade after decade, baseball cards were tortured by young kids and then executed and buried by their parents. How any of these cards survived the cardboard inferno is a minor miracle, but some did. They hid for years in shoeboxes in attics and closets. The few collectors over the age of 12 who actually ever looked at these mini-hoards never admitted doing so while in polite company. Sure, it was fine for a youngster to spend a few cents or a nickel on a wax pack, but for an adult to actually go out and spend money on a baseball card would have been viewed as something perilously close to aberrant behavior.

Sometime around the early 1970s, small bands of peculiar people began to gather. More often than not, it was in the privacy of someone's home, and every so often the brave ones would gather in a public place, like a library meeting room. These individuals were doing something their mothers, bankers, doctors, lawyers, and loved ones simply would not understand. They were meeting to trade, discuss and *buy* baseball cards. For years, these cardboard pioneers kept a relatively low profile, and with good reason. What would the neighbors think?

To obtain new cards, they would dash into a store, grab a handful of wax packs and mumble something to the clerk like,

"They're for my son," then dash home without ever letting on they had no son. The cards were for their own collections, and those collections were growing rapidly.

At about the same time, some of these pioneers realized a uniquely American thought. They reasoned, "If I've got something you want, and you'll pay me good money for it, I can go into business selling it." A few people did go into business, and in the process they were doing something adult males are not widely noted for doing; they were giving birth—to the baseball card market.

In the early 1970s the market wasn't much. Every so often, people would get together and sell cards to the few who were willing to be publicly seen buying baseball cards. To get new cards to sell you'd take out an advertisement in a local newspaper offering to buy (or more likely, come to someone's house and pick up) old baseball cards. Some people might call just to find out what sort of character would take old baseball cards. The pioneer baseball card dealer would come, cart away the cards, and perhaps even pay a few dollars for them. The former owners would chuckle at the genial "garbageman" who required an appointment and actually paid for the fun of picking up dust-collecting junk. The dealer probably chuckled a bit, too, as he carried away the Ruths, the Cobbs, the Mantles, and everything else.

Over the course of a few years, an odd thing happened. More and more people braved public scorn and started buying baseball cards. It wasn't the sort of thing you'd put on your resume, but it was fun, and amazingly, prices started going up. In 1979, Dr. Beckett published his first price guide, and the days of the 25 cent Mantle card quickly came to an end. (Now, Beckett sells about 80,000 copies of the annual *Sport Americana Baseball Price Guide,* and twice that many of his small, but mighty thick price guide of modern cards.)

Call it second childhood waiting to happen, call it retarded growth, or call it genius, the fact is that during the 1970s more and more people started buying and selling baseball cards. As they did, prices started climbing, even going so high that they would fall because of "market corrections." A dip in price here or there really did not bother most people, except for dealers, because most buyers were not investing in cards, just collecting them. Baseball cards were not the sort of thing for which you would mortgage your house or go to the limit on your credit cards. They generally were cheap and you spent money on them you never expected to see again.

Despite the growth, many adults still really couldn't understand why a few of their friends would actually spend money on baseball cards, or waste their weekends going to card shows. But the people who took part in these activities shared a common feeling that these things were "neat." They loved owning cards, felt proud of their collections, and were pleasantly surprised and perhaps even mildly amused when their cards started to rise in value.

Even in a sluggish market, like the early 1980s, there were signs of potential. Attending a baseball card show could be like a day on the commodity exchange with frantic buying, enormous enthusiasm, and lots of young faces. Some families had discovered that a card show was a nice way for everyone to spend time together.

In addition, card collecting publications were blossoming. What once had been a near void of information on cards and their prices was rapidly being filled. A few publications were even starting to appear on book and magazine shelves in major stores. You could go to the grocery store and right next to your favorite magazines find a Mickey Mantle baseball card on the cover of *Baseball Cards Magazine*. Dr. Beckett's annual price guides and his *Beckett's Baseball Card Monthly* magazine experienced tremendous growth in readership. Weekend shows started booming, dealerships were multiplying, and any American with so much as a casual interest in baseball cards was getting regular exposure through shows in conjunction with baseball teams, the use of cards on televised national broadcasts, and regular references to their values.

While some people were slightly shocked at both the new interest and the higher prices, many recognized it for what it was—just the tip of the iceberg. There were still relatively few cards priced at $100 or more, and very few at the $1,000 level. Baseball cards were still basically cheap, and the hobby was rapidly gaining respectability.

By the mid-1980s, more than the tip of the iceberg was visible. Dealers started noticing big increases in business. Subscriptions to baseball card magazines continued to grow at a steady or rising pace, and their advertising volume, reflecting the number of dealers and the card market, grew even faster. Prices were starting to move at a quicker pace as the new faces which were appearing in the marketplace placed a strain on the supplies of cards. Topps was now in fierce competition with Donruss and Fleer for the new cards sold in the market, and baseball cards were appearing everywhere.

Now, at the end of the 1980s, cards have enjoyed a popularity, even respect, that many of the pioneers would have never dreamed possible. And, of course, nothing breeds success like success. Dramatic price jumps became news, not just in the hobby, but also in the general news media. Newspapers like the *New York Times*, television programs like ABC's 20/20, magazines like *Newsweek* and *Sports Illustrated*, informed their audiences about the excitement, the fever, the potential for profits. The press coverage brought even more people into the hobby as collectors or speculative investors. No stocks, no bonds, no rare coins, virtually nothing could match the price performances of something like a rookie Dwight Gooden or Mark McGwire card. Sure, they might cost only a few dollars each, but investors look at percentages and that's where baseball cards put many other collectibles and investment vehicles to shame.

It's not just the prices that have produced the enormous growth, although it sure doesn't hurt a person's enthusiasm to see their cards double in price in three months. The millions of dollars in free publicity, the close ties to major league baseball, the major retail stores offering their own card sets, major companies such as Coca-Cola, True Value Hardware, and Kraft (Macaroni & Cheese Dinner) using cards as sales promotion tools all translated into one of the most dramatic and extensive sales efforts any hobby had ever seen. You simply could not escape the message: You should have baseball cards!

The most dramatic change, other than perhaps the price changes, was the public attitude about baseball cards. Those early pioneers who were bold enough to meet in public became the grandfathers of what has almost become a trendy thing to do. From an activity you didn't talk about in public, baseball cards became very nearly a badge of honor. That's where we are today, a hobby riding the crest of a boom few could envision less than a decade ago.

If history, indeed, does repeat itself then baseball card collectors may be viewing a re-run of 1964. Back then, though, the key players were coins, not cards.

There are striking similarities between the "panic buying" of the 1963-64 rare coin marketplace and what has been happening the past few years with cards. Just as the events of the 1960s caused happiness and despair, profits and financial losses, the current events with cards probably also will be all of the above—and be surprisingly beneficial to the hobby in the long run.

In the early 1960s there was rapid growth in "coin collecting." A few promoters repeatedly offered for sale large quantities of "scarce" items and their customers repeatedly purchased them. And they weren't just buying individual coins, they bought them in quantity by the rolls and even by the bags. Dozens or even thousands of the same kinds of coins were snapped up by each purchaser.

Often these rare coins were not really that rare at all. The purchases often consisted of rolls of rather common Franklin half dollars minted from 1948 through 1963, rolls of silver dollars that had been struck in the late 19th and early 20th centuries, and anything else that was "bright and shiny" and available in large enough quantities to heavily promote.

The more the promoters promoted, the more the general public bought. The more the public bought, the higher the prices went. About the only thing not being consumed in large quantity was knowledge. Only a relatively few of the new buyers did any serious studying of coins in either the hobby periodicals or numismatic books. The most common studying was the frequent close examination of price guides to determine how much profit the buyer had made in the last month or week.

Stories about coin collecting soon were not confined to the pages of hobby publications. News about the demand for "rare coins" and the quick profits they generated were carried in the daily newspapers, the *Wall Street Journal*, the nightly television newscasts. With so much positive publicity, more eager buyers entered the marketplace, and prices continued to rise.

There were collecting fads back then, too, like Lincoln cents and government-issued proof sets. Stamp collectors enjoyed plate blocks, the section of stamps from a whole sheet that carried the sheet's printing number(s) in the margin(s). People still collect these things today, of course, but no one is fighting in the streets for them. Instead, big money is going into such areas as high-quality gold coins and nice condition early, classic U.S. stamps. Many baseball card collectors today follow the fad of buying only current rookies. We think that trend will change, too, just as other hobbies have changing fads.

The rare coin market boom finally went bust around mid-1964. Too many of the promoters suddenly stopped buying large quantities of coins when they ran out of new customers and the artificially high prices plunged.

The collectors who made their purchases relatively early in the cycle and who sold their coins before the market fell made superb profits. Rare coins were a fabulous investment for them. But for the buyers who entered the market in early 1964 and were still holding their purchases when the merry-go-round stopped, it would be a long time before they could sell their coins at a profit. The next rare coin boom would not come until the early 1970s, and even then some of those coins would not reach their previous high values until another bull market in 1978-80. Some buyers of lower-quality material still have not been able to make a profit even with the latest numismatic boom market of 1988 where the emphasis has been on superb quality items.

The good news is that the big booms of 1964, 1973, 1978-80, and the current upturn in the rare coin marketplace each have brought new collectors into the hobby. When the speculators, hoarders, and investors fled elsewhere, some fresh faces remained; people who enjoyed the coins for their art, history, and romance—not just potential profits.

Notice the similarities? In today's baseball card marketplace there are buyers scrambling to accumulate factory-sealed cases containing thousands of assorted cards, cases that remain unopened and stashed away; there are buyers who prefer snapping up a hundred or even a thousand copies of the same player's card; and there are some unknowledgeable card buyers who might not know Vanna White from Whitey Ford.

However, there is a major aspect of the baseball card market that generally is not found in the rare coin and stamp markets, an aspect that is rarely discussed in public. It is the racial bias factor.

Racial bias apparently has held down the values of older cards of black super stars such as Jackie Robinson (1956 Topps #30) and Hank Aaron (1961 Topps #415).

(Copyright Topps Chewing Gum, Inc.)

The cards of black baseball players usually do not command the prices of comparable white players.

Explained dealer Al Rosen, "In the same sets in which Mays and Mantle appear, the Mantle card is worth five to ten times more than Mays. It's the same thing with Bob Gibson and Hank Aaron, and I think Aaron was about as good a ballplayer as Mantle and Mays. There are frankly very few black collectors, perhaps that's one of the reasons for the disparity."

Another dealer, who asked not to be identified by name, claimed the market has been much better for "white home run hitters" over the years.

Dealer Tony Galovich sees a changing attitude because of the interest in cards by young collectors. "The racial bias is in the older card buyers, the adults who see things in black and white. The young kids do not. They buy a Dwight Gooden card and don't look at him as a black player; they see him only as a super star pitcher. The racial factor is a problem with older collectors and dealers, but young kids coming into the hobby today don't see that.

So, I think the situation is changing, in fact, the Mays and Aaron cards are starting to slowly and surely catch up with the Mantle cards."

Although cards have been around for a century, the baseball card marketplace is still in its infancy.

With so many coin and stamp dealers now involved in the card marketplace, chances are very good that the house of cards will be built along the same lines as the patterns long-established in the buying and selling of postage stamps and rare coins. Gradually there will be more emphasis on research and rarity, more attention on the classic cards such as early Topps and Bowman, the Goudey cards of the 1930s, and the tobacco card issues, and more attention to grading with emphasis on top quality condition. And, yes, there will be market cycles, such as the current high one, followed by low periods of quiet enjoyment without as much of the frenzy of rapidly-rising prices for cards that are produced by the billions.

The crystal ball outlook: The card mania merry-go-round eventually will slow down, maybe even almost stop for a while, but the card collecting hobby will long endure; it already has. Those who enjoy their cards over the years as collectibles, not merely as a scheme for quick riches, should profit both in enjoyment and pocketbook.

The House of Cards

Why not all HOFers are created equal.

Investing in baseball cards can be very different things to different people. For some, it can be the purchase of 10,000 cards of one particular rookie at 10 cents each in the hope that the player will defy the odds and become a major star. If that happens, the $1,000 investment might become $10,000 in a few months.

In another instance, a baseball card investment might be a carefully selected Babe Ruth card. While spectacular gains might be unlikely, the Ruth card also is unlikely to drop significantly in price while the 10,000 exactly-the-same rookie cards could very quickly turn the original $1,000 investment into only $100.

Baseball card investing need not be expensive. A couple dollars spent on an unopened 1985 wax pack also represents an investment, just a very small one. A pack of commons could turn the two dollars into 50 cents, but a Roger Clemens rookie card might make your two dollars into a ten dollar bonanza.

Whatever your budget, or state of

nerves, baseball card investing offers opportunities for profits and losses that are every bit as real as money spent on Wall Street.

Although baseball cards have been around for more than 100 years, the notion of investing money in these bits of cardboard that once simply came as a premium in certain tobacco or candy products is relatively new. Before making a decision on what baseball cards would make good investments it is important to first understand what makes a card valuable.

If the cards you are considering are issues of the past few years, then the major price factor—other than condition—is demand. For recent cards, demand is centered on the rookie issues. In the 1987 Topps set it was the Mark McGwire card that soared to around seven dollars, not the Gary Carter which could be found readily for a quarter. That is not because McGwire is a better player than Carter, nor are there fewer of his cards. It is just that McGwire's is a rookie card. If you pick the right rookie, your profits will soar.

In the case of cards produced before the 1980s, a wide range of factors play a role in determining the future of a card's price. While the future of a current rookie's card is determined primarily by what the player does on the field, Babe Ruth will not hit any more home runs and "Marvelous" Marv Throneberry will be unable to raise his lifetime .237 average no matter how many beer commercials he appears in. (More later about how beer commercials have played a role in raising the value of another former player's cards.) Generally, for older cards the price variables of the player's abilities and fame are fixed.

However, a number of factors will have a profound effect on the future price of a card, be it a 1963 Pete Rose rookie or a T-206 Ty Cobb.

The first factor is rarity. As noted before, until the early 1970s, cards with higher numbers on them were produced in smaller quantities than cards with lower numbers. Hence, even common cards with higher numbers have higher price tags compared to the lower numbered commons of equal condition. For example, in the 1955 Topps set the high numbers begin at #161. As the following chart indicates, the lower numbered cards produced in much larger quantity always have sold at a fraction of the price of the 1955 Topps cards with numbers higher than #160.

1955 Commons
Low and High Numbers

1955	C1-150	C161-210
1981	$0.75	$2.50
1982	0.75	2.50
1983	0.75	2.50
1984	0.75	2.50
1985	0.75	2.50
1986	1.00	3.00
1987	2.75	5.50
1988	5.00	9.00

While rarity is a factor, it is not the only factor that might affect the future value of a card. The most valuable card in almost every collector's mind is the pre-World War I T-206 Honus Wagner. As mentioned earlier, the popular story behind the card is that Wagner objected to being associated with smoking and vigorously demanded that his (tobacco) card be removed from distribution. A relatively small number of the T-206 Wagners did get out. The number of this prized rarity known to exist today ranges from estimates of 40 to 60. That certainly makes it a scarce card, but many others are both scarcer and less expensive.

The T-206 Wagner brings tens of thousands of dollars (and in one case, more than $100,000) despite being almost common compared to some other cards because of the most basic form of supply and demand. Virtually everyone who has collected baseball cards for more than a few months probably would like to own one of the well-known Wagners.

Baseball cards are not alike. They can be attractive and they can be plain. Some contain excellent information while others may have nothing beyond the player's name and team affiliation. Such factors, coupled with the collectibility of the entire card set, can be extremely important when it comes to a card's future price because they are ingredients that influence the demand for the card. We can not overemphasize the importance of the demand part of the equation. In the case of the T-206 Wagner, not only is this card famous, it also is part of the most actively collected, pre-World War II set of tobacco cards. Place a T-206 card next to a T-207 in a dealer's display case and more often than not, the T-206 will sell first because it is much more attractive. (We also can not understate the importance of attractiveness or "eye appeal.")

An assortment of other considerations also can have a significant effect on the demand for a set. Price is perhaps the most important. As a card progressively goes up in price, the number of buyers with the resources to purchase the card is reduced. This applies to older cards as well as recent ones. The climb in price of a Don Mattingly rookie card slowed, not because Mattingly was having a bad season or because the demand for his cards had dropped off, but rather because the public's demand for paying $85 for the 1984 Donruss (#248) rookie Don Mattingly cards dropped at a time when some owners probably were attempting to take their profits. As a result, although the card market was soaring from 1987 to 1988, the Mattingly rookie Donruss card fell in retail value from $85 to $65. It was a simple case of supply and demand with the demand reduced due to the price, and the supply perhaps increasing for the very same reason.

As a general rule of thumb, if you are going to invest in baseball cards, the cards should be from a popular set. In the case of older tobacco cards, the best choices are T-205 and T-206. In the 1930s, the names to remember are Goudey and the Play Ball set that ran from 1939 to the early 1940s.

In 1948, the Bowman Gum Company issued the first of its card sets which are popular with collectors today as the source of "rookie" cards for many of the major players of the following decade. In fact, the 1951 Bowman set with rookies of Mickey Mantle, Willie Mays, and Whitey Ford must rank as one of the better sets of all time.

For the investor, nothing quite rivals the enormously popular and valuable Topps set of 1952. Since that time, Topps has been going strong and is usually considered the set of choice of most investors, something that is particularly true if your investment is in large lots of current rookie cards. Today, Topps faces more challenges for collector and investor dollars than at any time in its history. Donruss, Fleer, and Score sets are all worthy competitors, and of course, there are many other regional and promotional sets of cards being issued each year. There is no overall shortage of possible sets and cards on which to spend your money. The crucial decision is determining what you really want to buy.

While many other cards are interesting, historical and highly collectible, for an assortment of reasons the major brands most widely saved by both collectors and investors are the "Big Three" of Donruss, Fleer and Topps, and perhaps the "Big Four" with the new Score cards being added to the popularity of the three other sets.

Popularity of a given card can influence price, and more often than not, the greater the popularity, the greater the liquidity of your investment. It is currently popular to compare baseball cards to everything from rare coins and antiques to stocks. While prices of cards go up and down like the others, the comparison really is not terribly valid, although, as we mentioned before, some of the changes and trends already experienced in the stamp and coin fields already are being felt in the baseball card marketplace. One reason is that some stamp and coin dealers have entered the field.

No responsible financial analysts would suggest that you take your life savings down to the nearest dealer's shop or card show to buy all the Pete Rose rookies you can find. It's not that they don't like Rose; they would certainly feel the same way whether the cards were Babe Ruth or Jose Canseco rookies. Such cautious advice would be correct, for baseball cards, while a delight to own and enjoy, are not now—nor should anyone expect them to later become—a major investment vehicle for the prudent investor.

The reasons are many. The first point you must consider is that baseball cards have a very limited financial history. People have invested in stocks, bonds, real estate, precious metals and other commodities for decades if not centuries. The baseball card market we see today is an infant. It may be new, exciting, and at times spectacular, but it hardly has the sort of historical track record that justifies spending anything other than the spare funds you can afford to lose.

One of the difficulties found in baseball card investment is the matter of liquidity. Simply put, once you've purchased 10,000 precious John Kruk cards and they've soared from 20 cents to 75 cents each on the basis of his impressive rookie season, where do you go to sell them so you can realize your rather quick profit?

The truthful answer is: Almost nowhere.

While there probably are a lot of dealers who will buy 100 or maybe even 500 to 1,000 of the cards at a time, there are very few who have ever actually purchased such a quantity from a private individual, except in deals involving unopened cases of cards. The result is that the owner starts selling the large quantity of the player's rookie cards in groups of 100 cards here and another 300 there. In most cases the price will be dropping from the highest advertised buying prices to progressively lower values as the seller seeks out more buyers.

Liquidity can also be a problem with older cards. The collector-based market reflects the needs of collectors, and if your cards fall outside of the items with the highest demand your problems in liquidating these cards increase. The highest demand is found for Hall of Fame members' cards that are in already popular card sets. Again, a Topps 1957 Mickey Mantle or any of the T-206 Ty Cobb cards are relatively easy to sell, and at fair prices, too. However, if you have a less well-known member of the Hall of Fame on your tobacco card, or your 1957 Topps is not Mantle but a low-grade common card, liquidity gets tougher. And, the low-grade common of an unpopular card set can be very difficult to sell at anything close to the current value listed in a retail price guide.

The liquidity factor is important not just in selling your cards, but also in receiving a fair price for them. Remember that by the standards of many investments, baseball cards have a very high profit margin for the dealer selling them. This is not to suggest the profit is unfair, rather this is just to point out that the $7 you spend on a Gregg Jefferies card may represent only $3 to $4 if you attempted to sell it right away. To break even on the card it probably would have to go to $10 or more retail, and at that price buyers might well get very nervous because it went so high so quickly. Basically, to make a profit your cards must at least double in value. If you have problems selling them, you can cut your profit margin, or perhaps turn them over at a loss just to get cash and get out of the investment.

A final factor of concern in considering a baseball card investment is that they must be properly stored. The stock certificate you receive when you buy shares of a company is easily stored. You don't have to worry about it being folded, creased, or having its corners slightly bent, it will still be worth "X" amount of shares. Gold coins are easy to store. They can withstand thousands of years of contact with the natural elements and still look nice. A house can retain or increase its value with people living inside. But baseball cards are not that easy to preserve. They're made of rather flimsy cardboard, and large collections of them take up lots of space.

If you bought 10,000 Sam Horn rookie cards, you already are aware of the problems. And, if you spill cola, coffee, or cough syrup on them you can wipe out any potential profits in an instant. Cards don't withstand the natural environment anywhere nearly as well as a thousand year old gold coin. We've never heard of a pristine condition baseball card being successfully salvaged from an ocean shipwreck.

Even if you carefully preserve those cards, there are "natural disasters" in the marketplace, too. It might seem funny, but almost everyone who has invested in the hot rookie players of any given year learns that some of the cards will become almost worthless commons, and the commons tend to accumulate. First filling shelves, then closets, then entire rooms. Good investments gone bad, but still taking up space.

To avoid the problems associated with baseball card investment it's important to understand both baseball and the baseball card market. History can help in a limited way, for although we are barely past the stage where people tossed out their cards because they outgrew them, or just gave them away to dealers who were willing to haul them off, there are some trends worth considering.

There is little question that the most impressive price gains take place in the rookie card market. A 1987 Mark McGwire (#366) which originally could be found in a pack of Topps cards purchased at the store for as little as 50 cents, quickly went to $4. The 1984 Topps Dwight Gooden (#42T) already was selling for $4.25 in less than a year of its release, but today it is $40. The problem is that even players who win Rookie of the Year honors are not certain future stars. Take Ron Kittle. His 1984 Topps card (#480) went to $2.75 that year. In 1988, that same card was retailing for about 25 cents, meaning you would be lucky to get even 15 cents from a dealer for your Kittle rookie cards.

Second on any list of impressive gains in cards are those picturing major Hall of Fame members, sometimes abbreviated as HOFers. "Major" is an important word here. Everyone knows names like Ruth, Cobb, DiMaggio, Mantle, and Mays. However, there are approximately 200 inductees in the Hall of Fame, and while just about everyone might want a Babe Ruth card, demand is far less for players like Addie Joss, Earl Averill, or even Luis Aparicio. Simply put, not all HOFers are equal in demand even though many collectors specialize in them.

The following chart shows the price trends of significant older cards and sets including four cards in the famous 1933 Goudey set. Lou Gehrig (#92) and Babe Ruth (#144) are legends, both as players and as baseball cards. Rogers Hornsby, while perhaps well known, is not quite in their class, and while not many people today may know the name Goose Goslin, he, too, is in the Hall of Fame. (That's Goose Goslin, not Rich "Goose" Gossage.) Clearly, the better known the HOFers, the better the price appreciation for his cards.

Two Year Trends of Major Players

Card Issue	Condition and Price		
1933 Goudey #92 Gehrig	NrMT	EX	VG
1987	450	292.50	198.50
1988	1,700	680	340
1933 Goudey #144 Ruth	NrMT	EX	VG
1987	550	357.50	181.50
1988	2,500	1,000.00	500.00
1933 Goudey Goose Goslin	NrMT	EX	VG
1987	32	20.80	10.55
1988	55	27	16.60
1933 Goudey Rogers Hornsby	NrMT	EX	VG
1987	100	65	33
1988	159	75	45
1933 Goudey Set	NrMT	EX	VG
1987	6,800	4,425	2,250
1988	18,000	7,200	4,500
1914 Cracker Jack Cobb	NrMT	EX	VG
1987	825	536.25	272.25
1988	1,100	550	330
1914 Cracker Jack Joe Jackson	NrMT	EX	VG
1987	800	520	264
1988	1,000	500	300

Card Issue	Condition and Price		
1914 Cracker Jack Branch Rickey	NrMT	EX	VG
1987	125	81.25	41.25
1988	160	80.00	48.00
1914 Cracker Jack Set	NrMT	EX	VG
1987	7,500	5,625	4,125
1988	15,000	7,500	4,500
1948 Bowman Berra	NrMT	EX	VG
1987	80	52	26.40
1988	175	70	44
1948 Bowman Musial	NrMT	EX	VG
1987	80	52	26.40
1988	225	90	56.00
1948 Bowman Set	NrMT	EX	VG
1987	775	500	250
1988	1,500	525	300
1948 Leaf Joe DiMaggio	NrMT	EX	VG
1987	400	227.50	115.50
1988	500	225	140
1948 Leaf John Wagner	NrMT	EX	VG
1987	110	71.50	36.30
1988	150	75.00	45.00
1948 Leaf Bob Feller	NrMT	EX	VG
1987	425	276.25	140.25
1988	550	275.00	165.00
1948 Leaf Set	NrMT	EX	VG
1987	8,000	5,200	2,640
1988	13,000	6,500	3,900
Diamond Stars Ted Lyons	NrMT	EX	VG
1987	27.50	17.90	9
1988	35.00	17.50	10.50
Diamond Stars Mel Ott	NrMT	EX	VG
1987	48.50	31.55	16
1988	65.00	32.00	19.50
Diamond Stars Bill Dickey	NrMT	EX	VG
1987	250	162.50	82.50
1988	325	162.00	97.00
Diamond Stars Set	NrMT	EX	VG
1987	6,500	4,225	2,145
1988	6,000	3,000	1,800

Card Issue	Condition and Price		
1952 Topps Mantle	NrMT	EX	VG
1987	3,300	2,145	1,089
1988	6,500	2,275	1,300
1952 Topps Reese	NrMT	EX	VG
1987	400	260	132
1988	450	225	135
1952 Topps Set	NrMT	EX	VG
1987	22,000	10,500	5,200
1988	36,000	12,600	7,200

The card of a HOFer or baseball legend is a relatively secure investment. As long as they are in Cooperstown, there probably will be demand for their cards, although in varying degrees. Some cards can be a flash in the pan, experiencing unusual or unexplainable demand for whatever reason. In the past few years, Mickey Mantle is one of those players whose cards almost have become a fad. Yet, while fads come and go, it is safe to suggest that there will continue to be extremely heavy demand for Mantle. The following chart compares selected Mickey Mantle cards with those of Willie Mays.

Mantle vs. Mays

EX-MT	Mantle 1951 Bowman	Mays 1951B	Mantle 1955B	Mays 1955B
1981	$ 395.00	$ 355.00	$ 34.00	$30.00
1982	350.00	300.00	27.50	26.00
1983	305.00	260.00	32.50	26.00
1984	299.00	255.00	33.50	26.00
1985	325.00	280.00	40.00	28.00
1986	400.00	305.00	60.00	28.00
1987	1,000.00	575.00	120.00	55.00
1988	4,700.00	1,100.00	325.00	80.00
VG	Mantle 1951 Bowman	Mays 1951B	Mantle 1955B	Mays 1955B
1981	$ 237.00	$ 213.00	$ 20.40	$18.00
1982	210.00	180.00	16.50	15.60
1983	180.00	155.00	19.50	15.60
1984	180.00	153.00	20.00	15.60
1985	146.25	126.00	18.00	12.75
1986	180.00	138.00	27.00	12.75
1987	311.85	189.75	39.60	18.15
1988	940.00	275.00	60.00	24.00

NRMT	Mantle 1956 Topps	Mays 1956T	Mantle 1962T	Mays 1962T
1981	$ 65.75	$ 33.00	$ 18.75	$14.50
1982	59.75	29.00	18.75	14.00
1983	57.00	29.00	18.00	13.00
1984	60.00	30.00	19.50	30.00
1985	70.00	34.00	26.00	16.50
1986	90.00	38.00	38.00	18.00
1987	200.00	75.00	90.00	45.00
1988	600.00	100.00	325.00	55.00

VG	Mantle 1965 Topps	Mays 1956T	Mantle 1962T	Mays 1962T
1981	$ 39.45	$ 19.80	$ 11.25	$ 8.70
1982	35.80	17.35	11.25	8.30
1983	34.25	17.35	10.75	7.80
1984	36.00	18.00	11.75	9.00
1985	30.00	15.50	11.75	7.50
1986	40.50	17.25	17.25	8.10
1987	59.40	24.75	29.70	14.85
1988	125.00	25.00	60.00	13.50

The cards are comparable in rarity and the two players are similarly comparable in ability and public recognition. Yet, the Mays' cards command considerably less money. This is an example of the racial bias some of the dealers noted earlier. While the racial factor may or may not continue, there is ample historical evidence to indicate that current Mantle and Mays prices are unusually far apart. Either the current trend will become permanent, or it will return to a more balanced level; Mays must go up in price, or Mantle must come down. Some early indications suggest it may actually be a combination of the two that ultimately will produce a better price parity between them, although the probability is that Mantle cards always will be worth more than those of Mays.

A recent classic case of marketplace fads involves a "good field, no hit" player named Robert George Uecker. He's better known as Bob Uecker, and he is better known today for his broadcasting career than his baseball playing days. A 1962 Topps Uecker rookie card (#594) currently is listed at about $120 while a Gaylord Perry (#199) of the same year is $55. The Uecker upward price movement has been dramatic. The following chart shows Uecker's 1963 and 1967 cards. His other cards have shown similar increases.

Bob Uecker

	1963—#126	1967—#326
1981	0.20	.15
1982	0.20	.15
1983	0.20	.15
1984	0.20	.17
1985	0.20	.15
1986	1.50	.75
1987	7.00	5.00
1988	25.00	10.00

Impressive gains, aren't they? In fact, Robert George Uecker, a familiar face on beer commercials; alias "Mr. Baseball," the guy who must be in the front row; alias George Owens, the employer of Mr. Belvedere of the television series of that name; and also Milwaukee Brewers sportscaster has a baseball card that has performed considerably better than he did on the playing field. Uecker had a career batting average of only about .200 and never started in more than 80 games a season, yet his card has outperformed Mantle, Rose, Mays, Stargell, and just about any other super star you can name. Outside the currently hot rookies, one of the best investments you could have made since 1985 is the purchase of a Bob Uecker rookie card.

Although this amazing price climb for Uecker cards is a nice bonus for their owners, television shows do get cancelled, beer commercials do come and go, and eventually Uecker will use up his moments in the public spotlight. It may be five or ten years, but eventually the fad will end, and when it does, Bob Uecker cards will fall back to the price levels where they belong; just like a hot rookie who suddenly—and permanently—returns to Earth on the field and falls in the price guides when it's discovered he can't hit a curve.

Two final groups of cards worthy of mention are the two extremes of the baseball card market, the Commons and the Classics. Both groups really give you some idea about hobby strength. The Classics often are big names of the game, the great rarities, and overall, the most desired of all cards.

While the following is only a partial listing, it gives you an idea

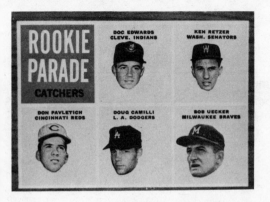

Bob Uecker obviously must be "in the front row" on his 1962 Topps rookie card (#594).

(Copyright Topps Chewing Gum, Inc.)

about the prices of some of the most desirable baseball cards during the 1980s. Most have done quite well, although weakness is seen in a few cases where the player or the card set fell slightly out of favor with today's collectors, or where the high price is simply too much for current marketplace demand.

Price Trends of Classics—EX-MT

	1981	1987	1988
T-206 Wagner	$17,500	$34,000	$36,000
1952-T Mantle	1,100	3,500	6,500
1951-T Stanky	2,500	2,275	2,275
1953-T Mays	675	600	950
T-207 Lowdermilk	750	1,350	1,700
1914-CJ Cobb	300	825	1,100
1968-T3-D Clemente	500	950	1,000
T-206 Maggie	750	3,100	5,500
1938-G Joe D	300	500	800
1933-G Lajoie	7,500	7,000	9,000
1954-T Aaron	175	350	500
T-207 Lewis	750	1,350	1,700
T-206 Plank	5,000	7,000	8,000
1954-B Williams	775	675	1,500
1933-G Ruth #144	250	550	2,500

The final group of cards is one where investment normally is not even considered, the commons. Commons are those everyday players who make up the majority of any major league team. The Jerry Roysters, Chris Speiers, Eddie Milners, and Joel Youngbloods of today, yesterday, and tomorrow. Generally, common cards only go up in value according to the popularity of the entire set of cards in which they were issued. For example, in near mint condition a common T-206 card has risen from about $4 in 1981 to about $30 today. In the case of the less popular E-120 American Caramel set, the rise has been from about $7 to $20 in the same time period. While normally not considered a good investment, if you pick a popular set sometimes the commons do better as investments than some big name players' cards in lower grade condition from another, but less popular set.

One more investment possibility can involve almost any card set prior to the 1960s. It is an investment factor that experienced collectors and investors call "condition rarities." The idea is to obtain one of the finest, if not *the* finest known example(s) of specific, scarce cards. Remember that baseball cards have no publicly-revealed production figures, and in some years certain cards were produced in larger quantities than others because of "double printing." As a result, not all cards of, say the 1955 Topps series, are equally available. There were larger quantities printed of some cards in the same sets. In mint or near mint condition, the situation can be even more complex because not all cards have been preserved equally.

A typical example is the 1952 Topps Andy Pafko card. It is the first card in the series that year and is very rare in mint condition. Apparently many youngsters of that era stacked their cards in numerical order and frequently held them together with a rubber band or two. The rubber bands dug into the #1 Pafko card. A number one card could sustain many other indignities, like having a soft drink spilled on the stack, splashing mostly on that top Topps card. Of the 1952 Topps cards, Pafko's took the worst beating. Finding one in superb mint condition may be quite difficult, barring the discovery of a hoard of unopened 1952 Topps packages.

Before you start spending big money on condition rarities, however, you want to be certain they actually are cards that are rare in top grades. Moreover, it's better if they are not widely known condition rarities. Pafko and the 1933 Goudey set's #1 card, Benny Bengough, are not exactly news to knowledgeable collectors, and their rarity in high grades already is reflected in their prices for nice specimens. Even a near mint condition Bengough can change hands at 30 times the value of a specimen in excellent condition.

If you're going to get involved in condition rarities, either you or your dealer had better really know baseball cards because unless you know what you're doing, you might very well spend too much on some card that isn't terribly rare at all, even in mint.

Well, obviously the options for investing are many. The big question now is, where should you put your money?

The Sudden Curve

Surely, there will be a burst of adjectives.

Unfortunately, a frank comment made by Bob Lemke, publisher of *Baseball Cards* magazine and *Sports Collectors Digest*, is just as appropriate today as it was when he said it in early 1986. "Unlike other collectible hobbies which have one fairly uniform set of grading standards, the baseball card hobby exists with nearly as many grading standards as there are collectors and dealers. No one, whether dealer or collector, is required to conform to any standard."

Despite the efforts of Lemke and others to improve the situation, various dealers and collectors still may greatly differ in their interpretations of grading "standards." Determining the condition of a baseball card is very subjective, but hobby leaders are diligently trying to seek common ground for defining different grades.

Both authors of this book have repeatedly warned for the past several years that as more rare coin dealers enter the baseball card marketplace and exert their influence, grading standards will become considerably stricter. For example, for generations, dealers and collectors described coins that did not exhibit any signs of wear as "uncirculated." If a really nice specimen were offered for sale, it might merit the additional adjective, "choice." But in the past two decades there have been tremendous changes in coin grading—both good and bad. Similar changes currently are happening with the grading of cards.

Rightly or wrongly, "precision grading" is a fact of life in coins and to some extent in stamp collecting-investing. It is "precisely" what is happening in baseball cards as the pattern is repeated. Coin dealer Maurice Rosen of Plainview, New York, accurately describes the efforts to achieve precision grading as "the grading Renaissance," but he also correctly notes that it has created a nightmare for many collectors, investors and dealers. Buyers who in good faith purchased "gem" (superb) quality items in 1979 have discovered that yesterday's "gem" may be only today's "choice" condition specimen—and with an appropriately lower value.

A generation ago, many postage stamp collectors simply affixed a hinge on the gummed back of most mint condition stamps so they could be mounted in an album. Today, stamps that have been hinged are worth less, sometimes much less, than comparable specimens that are accurately labeled "OG-NH," original gum-never hinged.

With stricter grading standards and increasing demand for only top quality items, baseball cards that show any stains from being packaged next to a stick of chewing gum or nestled against wax paper are definitely worth much less than similar cards that are free of these detracting marks. And, those mark-free cards must also have edges and corners that are not the slightest bit frayed or coming apart in layers.

There are problems with even widely-used, existing definitions. For example, many people in the hobby now say that a card with a gum stain can not be truly considered mint condition even if it just came out of the package. Does that almost automatically eliminate two-thirds of the early Bowman cards that came three to a wax pack with two of those three cards in direct contact with stain-producing pieces of bubble gum? Does that mean an otherwise pristine condition, well-centered, brilliantly colored, lustrous, sharp-cornered 1951 Bowman Roy Campanella card should sell

MONTE IRVIN

First Base—New York Giants
Born: Orange, N. J., Feb. 25, 1921
Height: 6-1   Weight: 195
Bats: Right   Throws: Right

Began 1950 with the Giants'
Jersey City farm team. In 18
games clouted 10 homers, batted in 33 runs, and piled up
a batting average of .510. He
was called up to the majors
in a hurry. In the lineup in
110 games for the Giants. Hit
an even .300. Drove in 66
runs. The 1950 season was
only Monte's second in organized baseball. In 1949 he hit
.373 in 63 games for Jersey
City; .224 in 36 for Giants.

No. 198 in the 1951 SERIES

BASEBALL
PICTURE CARDS
©1951 Bowman Gum, Inc., Phila., Pa., U.S.A.

Two kinds of value-slashing damage: a severely frayed corner with the cardboard separating into distinct layers, and two large chewing gum stains on the back of an otherwise very nice 1951 Bowman card of HOFer Monte Irvin.

for only $25 (the very good condition price) and not $250 because it has a gum stain on the back? By some definitions, cards with gum, wax, or other packaging stains are in the VG catagory, not higher. Obviously, there must be room for interpretation, refinement in definitions, and intermediate grades.

Until recently, virtually only one category existed to describe a baseball card that showed no signs of wear: Mint. But with more and more grading-conscious coin dealers entering the card market, and the continued increase of investors in the marketplace, there is no doubt that having just one category of "uncirculated" is grossly inadequate. Surely, there will be a burst of adjectives to describe better quality mint and near mint cards.

Choice, Gem, Superb, Spectacular, Dazzling, Sharp, and even "Wonder Card" are some of the terms we've either already seen or probably soon will be reading in hobby publications, price lists, and auctions. Of course, the better the adjective, the higher the price being asked for the card. There has been an unfortunate trend toward the use of plus and minus signs to denote grades. Among the absurd examples we've seen recently, a dealer listed a card as "EX+++" and another merchant who apparently could not bear to describe his wonderful card as being slightly worn and near mint offered it as "MT -." Both of those descriptions have appeared in various advertisements and are examples of ridiculous abuses of grading terminology.

We'll also probably see more use of split grades, giving separate grades to each side of the card. This can help both buyer and seller get a better picture of the card's true condition. A card easily could be labeled EX/VG, where the front grades excellent but the back is only very good. For example, an otherwise nice 1914 Cracker Jack card might have harsh stains on one side from coming in contact with the candy decades ago, and therefore could merit a split grade, such as EX/VG or VG/EX. But merely calling a single card VG-EX (with the two grades separated by a dash, not a slash) confusingly implies that its overall grade is in the entire range of very good to excellent. That kind of broad designation should not be tolerated; there just is too little precision and too much room for subjectivity. However, a seller in good faith can offer a series or set of cards as VG-EX because in that group of cards the individual items may range in grade from VG to EX. (You can bet the more expensive cards usually will be closer to VG than EX.)

Along the same lines, you can have a group of cards described as NR MT-MT, because some cards will grade near mint, others will be in mint condition. But watch out for any individual card labeled "NR MT-MT." If it's really near mint, then can it be mint? It can't. Period. Well, then, how is the NR MT-MT card priced? If a true mint example of that card is valued at $100 and a near mint specimen is $50, is something in-between a good buy at, say $60 or $90? You can argue that the grading label doesn't mean much as long as the card is appropriately priced for its actual condition. True, but a label can be misleading if you are not an expert on both grading and current card values. A designation of NR MT-MT for an individual card used to be quite acceptable when grading standards were much looser, but with today's grading Renaissance it no longer should be.

Dealers' increasingly critical eyes already are resulting in more demands for premium quality cards and tougher grading criteria. Look at the warnings some dealers boldly state in their advertisements to buy cards, "Strict grading essential to receive these prices. No off center or creased cards."

Remember, just a little difference in quality can mean a huge difference in price. The better the eye appeal, the greater the value of the card. As the trend for more precise grading takes hold the faintest hint of a crease, the most subtle dents and nicks, the slightest out-of-alignment printing, or the smallest trace of discoloration will lower the value of the cards. It might seem absurd compared to the casual atmosphere of card shows of years past, yet it is becoming increasingly common for many dealers to carefully examine higher-value cards under strong lighting with magnifying glasses; the same way dealers and collectors closely examine rare coins and postage stamps to determine their grades as well as authenticity. Don't be afraid to make that some kind of close examination when you are buying cards. After all, it's your money.

Now and then, a card that appears to be mint with excellent corners actually has been slightly altered. Previously damaged edges have been carefully trimmed. With the damage now removed, the card appears—at least at first glance—to be perfect. However, because it has been trimmed its value has been significantly shaved.

How serious is the problem of trimming? As the card market continues to grow the potential for this kind of abuse is tremendous. The idea is simple; since corners are an important part of grading, especially in top condition categories, sharp card corners tend to be worth good money. If someone has a valuable and attractive card in every respect except for the weak corner(s), a careful trimming will produce a sharp corner. While the card might appear a bit off center, in the normal course of business, a slightly off center mint condition card usually is worth more than a near mint specimen. For a quick, cautious trim, the person responsible might well be rewarded with an extra $1,000 when the card is sold to an unwary buyer. If you are the purchaser, you suddenly are the owner of a problem card, one that knowledgeable dealers will not buy from you even at vastly reduced prices because they simply do not want "tainted" cards in their inventories.

Several plastic measuring devices are now on the market to

help collectors and investors determine if cards have been trimmed. You just hold the card next to the gauge markings on the device and see if its length and width dimensions are correct for that card's particular year and series. These handy devices sell for less than $10 each, a small price to pay for an item that can save you 10, 100, or even 1,000 times that amount. If you don't have one of these gauges, consider purchasing one. Or, learn to use the no-gadget method successfully employed by experienced card buyers across the country: Just carefully hold one card next to a card in comparable condition from the same year and series to determine if their sizes are the equal. The comparison is best made with one of your own cards that you know is not trimmed. Why? Because if you compare the seller's suspicious card with others in the same sales display—and they *all* have been slightly trimmed— then they may all appear to be about the same size when compared with each other.

No matter how nice it looks, a card that has been trimmed is a problem card. A problem today, an even bigger problem tomorrow. Whether you are investing or collecting, a trimmed card is not something you should want, especially at the price levels you are likely to be asked to pay. Checking for the correct size takes only a few seconds, but it can be a potential savings of hundreds or even thousands of dollars. Do it.

When you are carefully examining a card for possible trimming, also look for signs of restoration. A few experts in the restoration of books and newspapers have been applying their skills to baseball cards, attempting to remove value-dropping creases and strains, and even sharpening card corners. Some of their work is deceptively good. Be very suspicious if an otherwise expensive card is offered for sale at considerably below the usual retail price. It may be a card with hidden problems. Remember, there is no Santa Claus in card collecting-investing. The only one laughing, "Ho, ho, ho," will be the person who successfully sold the restored, trimmed, and/or altered card to an unsuspecting buyer.

Another fact of life about grading is that no matter how wonderfully a dealer may have praised the condition of the cards you were buying from him, the chances are quite good that those cards won't appear quite as wonderful to some other dealer when you try to sell them a few years later. That's a frequent complaint of stamp and coin collectors and already is carrying over to the card marketplace, too. We have suggestions for dealing with those kinds of dealers in chapters 10 and 11.

Because of the increased attention to grading, and the growing distance between the value of a rare card in mint condition and the same card graded as only near mint, a few privately operated grading services have opened shop. Comparable to several businesses in the rare coin field, these companies offer to examine your cards and return them in individual, protective holders accompanied by certificates stating the grade of each card. Naturally, you pay a fee for each card certified by the grading service.

In the rare coin hobby, these services have helped buyers and sellers resolve differences of opinion on the condition of coins, and therefore, helped establish values for each certified item. However, not all grading services are created equal. Investors quickly learned that some services are either more liberal or more conservative in their opinions, and coins sometimes are priced not only by their certified grades, but also according to which certification service determined the grades.

That probably also will happen with baseball cards as more independent grading services enter the marketplace.

Although there are no uniform industry grading standards for baseball cards, several of the major hobby publishers have proposed ground rules for determining the condition of cards. Their grading definitions usually are printed in each issue of their magazine or newspaper. Read them carefully.

Recognizing the importance of accurate grading, and that excess subjectivity in grading standards can be reduced, each issue of *Beckett Baseball Card Monthly* magazine now is devoting two full pages to a very helpful, illustrated "Condition Guide." It even defines such terms as "minor defect" and "major defect." While we have some questions about potential confusion for readers with the magazine's price guide section (see chapter 12), Beckett's efforts at educating collectors about the realities of card grading deserve a grade of A-plus.

Krause Publications also provides readers of the company's various baseball card magazines and newspapers with grading

This 1983 Topps Ryne Sandberg rookie card (#83) shows the nice margins and four sharp corners of a mint condition specimen.

(Copyright Topps Chewing Gum, Inc.)

guides. Here are the word definitions used by Krause, along with photographs we've selected of cards that fit these categories. The first definition listed under each grade is from Krause's weekly *Sports Collectors Digest*, the second is from the monthly *Baseball Cards* magazine. Notice there are even slight variations in definitions among publications produced by the same parent company.

Mint (MT): A perfect card. Well-centered with all corners sharp and square. No creases, stains, edge nicks, surface marks, yellowing or fading, regardless of age.

Mint (MT): A perfect card. Well-centered with equal borders. Four sharp, square corners. No creases, edge dents, surface scratches, paper flaws, loss of luster, yellowing or fading, regardless of age. No imperfectly printed card—out of register, badly cut or ink-flawed—or card stained by contact with gum, wax or other susbstances can truly be considered Mint, even if new out of the pack.

Near Mint (NR MT): A nearly perfect card. At first glance, a NR MT card appears to be perfect. May have one corner not perfectly sharp. May be slightly off-center. No surface marks, creases, or loss of gloss.

This 1963 multi-player rookie card of HOFer Willie Stargell (Topps #553) would be mint, but a small bend in the upper right corner makes it only near mint.

(Copyright Topps Chewing Gum, Inc.)

Near Mint (NR MT): A nearly perfect card. At first glance, a Near Mint card appears perfect; under close examination, however, a minor flaw will be discovered. On well-centered cards, three of the four corners must be perfectly sharp. A slightly off-center card would also fit this grade.

Excellent (EX): Corners are still fairly sharp with only moderate wear. Borders may be off-center. No creases or stains on fronts or backs, but may show slight loss of surface luster.

Excellent (EX): Corners are still fairly sharp with only moderate wear. Card borders may be off center. No creases. No gum, wax or product stains, front or back. Surfaces may show some loss of luster.

Very Good (VG): Shows obvious handling. May have rounded corners, minor creases, moderate gum or wax stains. No major creases, tape marks, writing, etc.

Very Good (VG): Shows obvious handling. Corners rounded and/or perhaps showing minor creases. Other minor

Some dealers might label this card as "EX-NR MT," but when it's time for you to sell this 1940 HOFer Napoleon "Larry" Lajoie Play Ball card (#173) its true condition will be nearer to excellent than near mint because of the two rounded bottom corners.

crease may be visible. Surfaces may exhibit loss of luster, but all printing is intact. May show gum, wax or other packaging stains. No major creases, tape marks or extraneous markings or writing. Exhibits honest wear.

Good (G): A well-worn card, but exhibits no intentional damage. May have major or multiple creases. Corners may be rounded well beyond card border.

Good (G): A well-worn card with no intentional damage or abuse. May have major or multiple creases. Corners rounded well beyond the border.

Fair (F): A complete card, but contains damage such as writing on card back, tack holes, and heavy creases.

Fair (F): Shows excessive wear, along with damage or abuse, such as thumbtack holes in or near margins, evidence of having been taped or pasted, perhaps small tears around the edges, or creases so heavy as to break the cardboard. Backs may show minor added writing or be missing small bits of paper. Still, a basically complete card.

Four rounded corners put this 1954 Topps (#128) rookie card of HOFer Hank Aaron into the very good category.

(Copyright Topps Chewing Gum, Inc.)

Poor (P): (*Baseball Cards* magazine only) A card that has been tortured to death. Corners or other areas may be torn off. Cards may have been trimmed, show holes from a paper punch or have been used for BB-gun practice. Front may have extraneous pen or pencil writing or other defacement. Major portions of front and back design may be missing. Not a pretty sight.

Kit Kiefer, editor of *Baseball Cards* magazine, points out that in addition to the grades listed above "collectors will often encounter intermediate grades, such as VG-EX (very good to excellent), EX-MT (excellent to mint), or NR MT-MT (near mint to mint). Intermediate grades are used to indicate that a card has all the characteristics of the lower grade, with enough of those of the higher grade to merit mention. Such cards are usually priced at a point midway between the two grades."

It is possible that someday the hobby may adopt well-defined grading standards for different card series; for example, taking into account the differences between the paper and printing techniques used for specific early 20th century cards and the high-tech manufacturing procedures of the modern era. But for today, just make sure that if you pay a mint price you get a mint card, not one that only grades excellent or even near mint. And, just as carefully examine cards labeled very good to determine if they really are. No matter what the price, buying overgraded cards will make you feel *poor*.

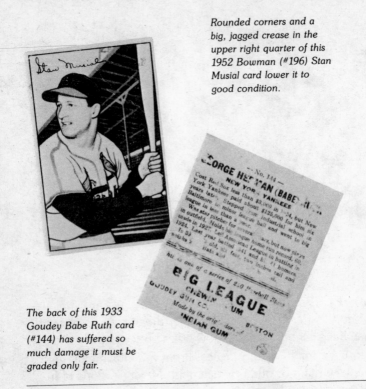

Rounded corners and a
big, jagged crease in the
upper right quarter of this
1952 Bowman (#196) Stan
Musial card lower it to
good condition.

The back of this 1933
Goudey Babe Ruth card
(#144) has suffered so
much damage it must be
graded only fair.

Old Timers Game

Investing in

pre-World

War II

cards

Who's on first? Who?
Never heard of him . . .

The baseball cards we know today have their roots in the trade cards of Great Britain. These were simply advertisements, cards generally given away with a specific product to help promote future sales. Shortly after the U.S. Civil War, trade cards became fairly common in the United States, although baseball players were not exactly a significant feature of these cards.

As early as 1868, cards were being issued with pictures of the major baseball teams of the day. Almost 20 years later, the first baseball cards to be widely distributed were produced (see chapter 2). It launched a fascinating era and another national pastime.

However, while many collectors may love these tobacco cards, investors might be slightly less excited about these and other historic issues of the 1800s for a number of reasons.

One problem is that many of the cards are difficult to find. Their rarity, along with relatively high prices, make them very marginal investments. Price trends over the last decade show very modest growth, if any.

Naturally, because of their age and the circumstances under which they were given away and stored over the years, many older cards today are in a condition that could gently be described as well below mint. The owners at the time they were issued were being given a simple novelty, not a valuable commodity that should be carefully cherished, collected, and preserved. Usually no great pains were taken to protect the sometimes fragile issues of the period.

Cards from before 1900 suffer as investments for several other reasons: Rarity in nice condition, difficulty in obtaining some cards in any condition, and frequently unattractive appearance in other instances all hurt these cards. But most damaging is the lack of interest and lack of knowledge about baseball and its stars before the turn of the century. Babe Ruth and Hank Aaron are household words, however, Hall of Famers (HOFers) like John Clarkson, Monte Ward, and Timothy Keefe are not, unless you have a lifetime pass to Cooperstown and use it frequently. The biggest names of the pre-1900 era, such as Cap Anson, are known by some today, while Charles Comiskey is known more for the old Chicago ballpark that bears his name than for being in the Hall of Fame.

In a sense it is sad that King Kelly and "Old Hoss" Radbourn who went 60-12 in 1884 are unknown to many. Unless there is a major increase in interest in their era and the cards of their time the price trends for 19th century cards will remain relatively flat when compared to recent cards.

The first few years of the 20th century passed without any significant new issues of baseball cards, but by 1910 the future trends already were well in place. Card production was heading in two directions. They were increasingly a part of cigarette promotions and were being produced by candy companies for use with their products. For two decades, the tobacco (T-cards) and caramel companies (E-cards) would dominate the market.

The investor or collector is confronted here with an almost bewildering array of cards from this period. Before spending any money, you need some background information. The reason is simple, just as with HOFers, not all Walter Johnson or Ty Cobb cards are created equal. The same for other major stars of the day.

As a general rule of thumb, tobacco cards are more valuable than other types of cards from the period. Even knowing that, all tobacco cards are not equal.

The big three of tobacco card sets are the T-205, T-206 and T-207 sets. As this book was being written, one of the authors was offered Walter Johnson cards in identical condition from the T-205 and T-207 sets. The author purchased only the higher priced T-205 card, even though the T-207 Johnson was very reasonably priced. In a short period of time, there were two opportunities to re-sell the T-205 for a profit; yet the dealer who originally offered the T-207 still had possession of that card even though he lowered his asking price. Finally, the dealer was able to sell the T-207 Johnson for $150. That was $30 below the amount he originally paid for it! This is an excellent example of what happens frequently because the T-205 is a much more popular early card set than the rather drab T-207 with its brown background color.

If a promoter obtained a huge assortment of these cards and began aggressively marketing them, it could increase demand and at least temporarily drive up prices. Similar things have repeatedly happened with some rare coins and postage stamps. However, when the promotion ends, the prices usually fall back quickly.

The following chart gives an indication of some price trends of selected 19th and early 20th century cards.

Price Trends of Selected 19th and Early 20th Century Cards

	1981	1987	1988
19th Century Trends			
N-28 (EX)			
Common	$50	$65	$75
Anson	200	390	400
Kelly	125	162.50	162
HOF	100	130	137
N-300			
Common	75	50	65
Anson	350	250	325
HOF	125	125-150	162-200
20th Century T-Cards			
T-203 Turkey Reds			
Common	40	81-113	62-75
HOF	75-200	146-390	125-300
Cobb	500	1,137.50	1,000
T-204 Ramly			
Common	60	52	62
HOF	125	113.75	150-200
Johnson	200	308.75	400
Plank	200	146.25	225

	1981	1987	1988
T-205 Gold Border			
Common	5	10	20
HOF	15-25	25-87.50	200
Cobb	150	200	450
T-206			
Common	4	9.75	15
HOF	15-35	23-81	37-162
Cobb	100-150	195-292	350-500
20th Century E-Cards			
E-120 American Car.			
Common	7	9.75	10
HOF	15	19-48	20-75
Cobb	75	130	250
Ruth	100	211.25	325
1914 Cracker Jack			
Common	25	29.25	30
HOF	45	45-211	45-212
Cobb	175	536.25	550
Mathewson	175	227.5	225
Chance	175	227.5	225

Except in the case of the major names such as Cobb and Ruth, the hobby staples, the T-205 and T-206 tobacco cards outperform other T and E-cards. That trend likely is to continue as even the attractive sets like T-204 and T-203 are "flawed" by their rarity, their price, and the lack of major players being depicted in the T-204 series and the unusual size of the T-203 cards. The American Caramel E-120 set is handicapped by the fact that the pictures are used on other caramel sets and the large number of cards needed to complete a set; yet it ranks as about the best of the caramel baseball card sets.

Looking at the issues of the early part of this century from an investment point of view is a complex task. Few could be considered anything close to common, especially when compared to issues of the past few years. While demand is very good for some players such as Ty Cobb, even lesser-known HOFers are relegated to the status of cards that primarily would interest only serious collectors of these early sets. Even so, the baseball card hobby has undergone tremendous expansion in recent years, and if just small numbers of the newcomers seek early sets or merely stars and

*A sometimes overlooked
Hall of Fame player,
Napoleon LaJoie, is shown
here on an E-92 series card
from 1909.*

HOFers from these early years, selected cards from these sets should do well. Even the commons should be relatively solid and secure places for your money under those circumstances.

The investors seeking the best places for their money in these early cards must start with Ruth and Cobb, the two dominant players of the era, followed closely by Lou Gehrig, Honus Wagner, Walter Johnson, and Christy Mathewson among others. As shown in the price charts, Ruth, Cobb, and Gehrig in particular have done extremely well in recent years, and competition remains fierce for nice quality examples of all three.

Even with a certain amount of speculation on those three, this trio amounts to the Blue Chip names of baseball before World War II. Investing in them is not, however, something that can be done merely by spending money on the first Ty Cobb that comes along. In the T-206 set there are four different Cobb cards, and unless you know whether you would rather have a Cobb portrait with a red background or one with a green background (which is more valuable), you probably should be buying Wall Street mutual stock funds and not Ty Cobb cards.

Knowledge in the case of older cards is extremely beneficial whether it is recognizing lesser-known HOFers or just lesser-known cards. Here's an example. Take a close look at the card on page 76.

No, it is not particularly attractive, and no, the condition is not very nice. On a grading scale of poor to mint condition, it grades close to terrible. But it is a Babe Ruth card. For many collectors it would not seem especially valuable, except to be purchased as a low-priced, low-grade Ruth card. Then why is there a waiting list of potential customers who want to buy this card for many times its last purchase price? The answer is: 1915. That's when the card was issued, and 1915 is the first full year in the major leagues for a young pitcher named George Herman Ruth. The authors have seen only a few of these cards advertised in the past few years, and while it is still not the most costly Babe Ruth card it is typical of older cards that might just have some added potential.

Rookies, the highest-flying, most avidly-sought cards being produced today, are either unknown or virtually ignored in the cards from the early part of the 20th century. With some research you can arm yourself with information (when it is available) on early rookie cards, so the next time you have the chance to buy a 1910 Old Mill card of Casey Stengel you'll know it is not any old Stengel, it is his rookie card using today's definition. For a little bit of extra money these kinds of cards certainly are an interesting investment.

For those looking for another option involving older cards, a strategy that can work is to obtain examples of players having a

A surprise addition to Cooperstown in 1986 was Bobby Doerr, shown on a 1941 Play Ball card (#64).

chance to get into the Hall of Fame through the 20 member "old timers" committee, officially called The Baseball Hall of Fame Committee on Baseball Veterans. It does not take Cagney and Lacey's detective skills to identify these players. In fact, there is speculation in the sports media each year about the five to ten top candidates. If you have a subscription to the *Sporting News* and have a baseball encyclopedia you almost certainly can come up with your own list of likely names. Some players, such as Enos Slaughter, are already priced at nearly Hall of Fame levels by the time they are selected for the Cooperstown honors. Others, such as the 1986 selection of Bobby Doerr, come as something of a surprise to many sports fans and collectors. It certainly did not hurt the value of the investments made by those collectors who correctly anticipated that when former teammate Ted Williams became a member of the old timers group it would help Doerr's Hall of Fame chances.

One player who deserves special mention under the "might make the Hall of Fame" category is Shoeless Joe Jackson. Possibly the greatest player ever, Jackson was banished from baseball after the 1919 World Series (the Black Sox scandal). If his name were cleared, and there are efforts being made toward that because of the controversial way his case was handled, Jackson's posthumous induction into the Hall of Fame virtually would be automatic.

However, he would not be a surprise. The few card varieties picturing him already are at high levels because of strong demand.

Even at their current levels, Shoeless Joe Jackson cards may be a good deal. He looms larger than life in his banishment. Movies, television programs, books, and public fascination about Jackson continue 70 years after the disputed World Series. As long as that fascination continues, he will probably remain the most valuable and desirable card of those players not currently active in the game or already in the Hall of Fame.

Under the "sleeper" category for early cards, and certainly related to those of Joe Jackson, are the cards of Buck Weaver, the only other member of the 1919 Chicago White Sox team who has a chance to have his name cleared of any wrongdoing in the Black Sox bribery case. As the premier third baseman of his day, Weaver would also be a likely Hall of Fame choice.

From the Goudey Gum Company's 1933 240 card set until the arrival of the first Bowman cards in 1948 there were many interesting sets that include a lot of valuable cards. As with players before 1933, information is the key here. Potentially important, but overlooked compared to something like a Pete Rose rookie, are the rookie cards of such players as Joe DiMaggio, Ted Williams, Bob Feller, and others whose first cards are found in the sets of this era.

The highest priced and most speculative cards of the period are the big names—Ruth, Gehrig, DiMaggio, and even a Shoeless Joe Jackson card that is part of the 1940 Play Ball set; although these Jackson cards usually are found today damaged or even defaced. Relatively cheap and safe HOFers cards exist in abundance ranging from Carl Hubbell to Heine Manush to Chuck Klein.

When considering investment in older cards, remember that higher grade cards, especially mint condition if you can find them, are the best. Once you drop in condition to excellent, the potential for future increase in value drops off to a point where there is very little difference between a player's card in excellent or very good. In fact, there is even some price trend evidence that the more affordable VG's have appreciated slightly better than the slightly worn, excellent condition cards.

In many instances, when it comes to grading, the collectors have an advantage over the investors because they can always acquire an example of a card and fill a hole in their collection until they can trade up for a better specimen when one becomes available at a later date. That becomes a real consideration in early cards where it's extremely rare for them to exist in mint condition or anything even remotely close to mint. In assembling a set of the popular 1933 Goudey cards, which seems to have survived a half century in many cases in nice condition, waiting for a mint or near mint Babe Ruth may be no problem. But with the 1915 Ruth rookie card the situation is vastly different because the best condition available may be only excellent. And you'll probably wait a year or more just to find one that good—at any price.

Many investors might feel that older cards offer little potential for growth, but nothing could be further from the truth. From 1987 to 1988, a near mint Goudey #144 Babe Ruth rose from $550 to $2,500. Even in VG, the same card went from $180 to $500.

There are risks in older cards, but in reality probably fewer risks than in buying 300 Greg Swindell rookie cards. Instead of learning minor league batting averages, investors (and collectors) need to learn about former greats, potential HOFers, and a wide range of interesting, valuable, and sometimes beautiful baseball cards.

Baby Boomers

Investing in

post-World

War II

cards

Why Bob Uecker must be in the front row.

What an era! There were Willie and Mickey and the Duke. The Yankees dynasty, the Boys of Summer, Stan the Man, Ted Williams, and so many more. A truly golden era, and one that still can pay off in gold today if you happen to have the right cards.

The end of World War II saw the beginning of the modern era of baseball cards. It started with some minor issues, then burst forth in 1948 with the first Bowman and Leaf cards. By the late 1970s, the only name you needed to know in cards was Topps.

Whether you're 40 or 14, these are the cards of your youth, the cards you flipped against walls, attached to bicycle spokes, and which eventually were thrown out during spring cleaning. If you want to buy them back, in some cases those old pieces of cardboard will cost about the same price as a car.

Is there money to be made in cards from 1948 to 1979? Consider the classic, the 1952 Topps Mickey Mantle card. It was listed at $3,300 in near mint condition in 1987. A year later, the asking price was $6,500. A

Roberto Clemente 1955 rookie card was $97.50 in 1981, but to-day is about $500. In the same time period the 1963 Mantle went from $28.50 to $250 in near mint, while a Pete Rose rookie of the same year jumped from $68.50 to $450. Bob Uecker went from just 20 cents to $25, and that's his 1963 card, not his 1962 rookie card.

Over the past few years, if you owned cards from this period the question was not whether they went up in value, the question was *how much* did they go up.

When you read some of the current promotions regarding baseball cards, the clear message is that nothing—not stocks, bonds, real estate, gold, or anything else—went up quite as quickly or as regularly as baseball cards. And, if you believe that, boy, have we got some cards for you!

Charts of baseball card prices starting with the year 1981 follow. The cards are from 1955, 1963 and 1967. Track their prices over that period and you'll find that, on the average, cards did increase in value, and when you compare their 1981 prices with those in 1988 you'll see the differences often are very dramatic.

Rookies, Stars, and Sets in NR MT
1955, 1963, and 1967 Topps

1955	Ted Williams #2	Sandy Koufax #123 (R)	Harmon Killebrew #124(R)
1981	$ 28.00	$ 29.25	$16.00
1982	27.00	30.75	15.25
1983	25.50	34.00	16.00
1984	26.50	35.00	17.00
1985	32.00	42.00	25.00
1986	40.00	60.00	35.00
1987	65.00	120.00	60.00
1988	150.00	250.00	90.00

1955	Roberto Clemente #164 (R)	Yogi Berra #198	Set
1981	$ 97.50	$ 34.75	$ 650
1982	85.00	31.25	625
1983	80.00	30.00	625
1984	87.00	30.00	630
1985	87.00	32.00	630
1986	95.00	32.00	730
1987	225.00	70.00	1350
1988	400.00	125.00	3750

1963	Mantle #200	Mays #300	Bob Uecker #126	Rose #537 (R)	Stargell #553 (R)
1981	$ 28.50	$25.00	$ 0.20	$ 68.25	$ 18.25
1982	27.50	21.50	0.20	120.00	18.25
1983	24.50	21.50	0.20	270.00	20.00
1984	25.50	22.50	0.20	285.00	25.50
1985	27.50	24.00	0.20	300.00	27.50
1986	38.00	30.00	1.50	345.00	30.00
1987	60.00	45.00	7.00	425.00	48.00
1988	250.00	60.00	25.00	450.00	110.00

1967	Mantle #150	Uecker #326	Rose #430	Carew #569 (R)	Seaver #581 (R)
1981	$ 12.00	$ .15	$ 9.50	$ 36.00	$ 74.25
1982	12.00	.15	12.00	38.25	70.50
1983	14.00	.15	19.00	34.00	70.50
1984	14.75	.17	23.50	40.00	73.00
1985	20.00	.15	29.00	65.00	85.00
1986	29.00	.75	30.00	85.00	130.00
1987	55.00	5.00	54.00	110.00	250.00
1988	175.00	10.00	65.00	125.00	400.00

Start first with the chart of 1955 Topps cards. From their 1981 high values, many fell over the next two years. The Roberto Clemente rookie card did not climb past its 1981 price until 1987. Remember, too, that retail prices often are 50 percent *more* than what you'll get when you sell your card to a dealer in the market, so it took the Clemente rookie card seven years to produce a roughly 100 percent return on investment.

While other cards did better, none did much better than break even for their owners from 1981 to 1986, and these are cards in better (higher) grades. In the very good condition columns things are even less encouraging.

Next, examine the near mint condition cards of 1963 and 1967. Here, the selected cards include rookies of Pete Rose, Willie Stargell, Rod Carew, and Tom Seaver, as well as non-rookie cards of Mickey Mantle, Willie Mays, and Bob Uecker. The Uecker card experienced a huge rise because it became a fad starting in 1986. The four rookies tracked here are among the best since 1960, and Mantle and Mays need no introduction to anyone. However, note that in 1982 and 1983, the Mantle and Mays cards actually dropped in value, while Uecker remained unchanged. Stargell was up slightly, and only Rose climbed significantly among the 1963 issues. In the case of the 1967 cards, during 1982 and 1983 the

Carew and Seaver rookies were down after the two years, Uecker was unchanged, Mantle was up slightly, and only Rose was up significantly. Hardly a bonanza, even though you could find few, if any better groups of cards from these sets.

When you factor in the potential 50 percent difference between the retail value and the dealers' actual buying price from a customer, few of these cards would have produced profits for their owners after five years, and many took six and some took the full seven years to do it.

Are there lessons to be learned from these price trends? One is that while baseball cards can go up, sometimes dramatically as is seen in the case of virtually all cards from 1987 to 1988, they also can go down. This is true not only for a rookie who looks like Don Mattingly one year but whose batting average is lower than Goofy's I.Q. the next, but also for such quality rookie cards as Mickey Mantle's or Tom Seaver's. They, too, can go down—an important lesson to remember.

In examining the cards of the period from 1948 to 1980 we find important characteristics for them and their prices. The first factor, and this cannot be repeated too often, is that the highest grades perform the best. The VG card may fill a hole in your collection and even may be readily saleable to an eager buyer, but chances are good it will not return the same profit margin as the truly mint condition card.

Cards from 1948 to 1980 require every bit as much study as those of the early days of baseball or the hot rookies of today. Consider the case of the Yogi Berra 1948 Bowman rookie card. It recently has been priced at about $200 in near mint condition. That may seem inexpensive, but it looks downright cheap when you realize that the 1953 Topps rookies of Jim Gilliam and Johnny Podres in the same condition are currently at about the same price level. Is everyone in the marketplace, including the price guide writers, totally crazy?

Not really. The 1948 Berra rookie is a Bowman, not a Topps. That cuts down on its popularity. There just are more collectors and investors who prefer Topps cards of that era. Also, the Berra card is not in color while the Gilliam and Podres cards are made by Topps, are in color, and are part of a set that is considered by some to be among the most attractive ever produced. In the Bowman set, the Berra card is one of the more common low-numbered cards, #6. The Gilliam (#258) and Podres (#263) cards are in the higher-numbered issues for 1953, and therefore, were produced in much lower quantity than the cards issued earlier that year with the lower numbers on them.

Perhaps the Berra rookie is underpriced while the Gilliam and Podres rookies are high, but the person who knows about cards and the card market is a lot less likely to assume that the prices are way out of line than the person who merely assumes that the cards are all equal. Knowledge of the cards is important, and so is knowledge of their current prices and their price history. The goal of any investor must be to buy low and sell high. Hitting the exact bottom or top of a price trend is desirable, but it actually is less important than being within 10 to 20 percent of the pricing extremes. Based on the 1987 to 1988 trends, baseball card peaks may be among the most difficult of all to sense, yet a knowledge of the marketplace will certainly help.

It seems that baseball cards have entered a period of extreme volatility. When prices double or triple in one year, understanding the market is more important than ever, for the moment demand starts to slacken, an upward price trend might well be over. If you bought a nice 1956 Mantle for $200 and they are now $650, should you be concerned about whether that card is near the top of its trend? Of course, and if you knew it was valued at only $90 the year before you paid $200 for it, you'd be even more concerned. After all, fewer people are willing and able to spend $650 than $200, and once the mob stops chasing a currently "hot" card it can turn very cold very quickly and its price can fall a long way before recovering. Your goal is to sell the overpriced cards to buy the underpriced ones. But if you get greedy in the process, you could find you are your own worst enemy.

Evaluating the 1948 to 1980 period you can find many interesting cards and opportunities. Starting with the Bowmans from 1948 through 1955, you can find a wealth of great rookies and seemingly underpriced cards. Although only a 48 card set, the 1948 Bowman set perhaps is the ideal place for starting a baseball card collection. When you evaluate the Bowman sets for investments there are some significant pros and cons. The biggest negative against Bowmans is that they are not Topps cards. They also are obsolete, as the last Bowman card was produced in 1955.

Other problems with the cards are their size; for many years they were smaller than the card sizes collectors and investors are familiar with today. Although this prejudice makes no sense to those familiar with the tobacco, caramel, and Goudey issues, in some minds a 1951 Bowman Mantle—his true rookie card—is not as desirable as his Topps card from the famous 1952 Topps set. While the logic, or lack thereof, behind these feelings against Bowmans can be questioned and refuted, the feelings are still real for many collectors and investors. On more than one occasion, one of the authors displayed very desirable Bowmans and perhaps less desirable Topps cards to people, and more often than not, even after the importance of the Bowmans is made clear, the people will explain they only want Topps cards and they just don't like those "little" ones.

Another problem (in some cases) is the appearance of Bowmans, the eye appeal factor. No question—the black and white pictures hurt the 1948 Bowmans just as they hurt the Play Ball sets of the early 1940s. The problem is not limited to the 1948 Bowman set. The 240 card 1949 set also is not very attractive, although color was added and it does have rookie cards of players like Robin Roberts, Duke Snider, Satchel Paige, Roy Campanella, and Richie Ashburn.

Even though Bowman produced some extraordinarily attractive and innovative cards from 1948 through 1955 which old timers in the hobby appreciate and desire, it appears that Bowmans are an acquired taste. They probably never will have the same demand as Topps, and it may be many years, if ever, before the newcomers both in the ranks of card collecting and investing start seeking some of the more important Bowman cards.

That said, it is important for the investor to understand some of the "sleepers" and significant cards issued by Bowman. Until Topps arrived on the scene in force in 1952, Bowman basically had the field to itself with the exception of 1948 when Leaf beat Bowman badly when it came to having big name players depicted on their cards. As luck would have it, the years of 1949, 1950, and 1951 were a good time for rookies. If you count the Yogi Berra rookie in 1948 before Topps really issued a regular card set, Bowman had produced rookie cards of most of the major players of the 1950s including Mantle, Mays, Ford and Monte Irvin, all in 1951.

Bowman also produced rather attractive cards including their 1952 and 1953 color sets. The 1955 Bowman set is distinguished not only by its television set design, but also by the presence of umpire cards.

Among the important cards found in Bowman sets is the Satchel Paige of 1949, technically the Paige rookie card and one of the most valuable of all Bowman items. Another significant name found in 1952 and 1953 Bowman sets is Stan Musial. His 1953 Bowman is the last time Musial appears on a nationally distributed bubblegum card until 1958, so you have to consider that Stan Musial Bowmans are very solid places to safely spend your baseball card money.

Yet another major Bowman card is the 1954 Ted Williams. These cards actually were withdrawn from distribution, probably because Williams signed a contract with Topps, in whose set he appears twice in 1954. Bowman apparently was forced to withdraw their #66 Ted Williams cards which they replaced with a #66 Jimmy Piersall. It has long been an item of faith that the Piersall is scarce and the Williams quite rare. While neither is especially common, the Williams card legitimately is not seen with great frequency; yet neither is as tough to locate as some in the marketplace might have you believe. Moreover, with its high price, the 1954 Bowman Ted Williams has not been an especially good investment during this last boom market, not even doubling in value. Now at the $1,800 level in near mint condition, it seems unlikely that it will do all that much better in the near future.

When Bowman was bought out by Topps in 1956, before Bowman could issue another set, it marked the end of a brief but glorious era when the two companies fought over both player and public loyalty. Had things turned out the other way, it probably would be Bowman cards that are universally sought today while Topps would be struggling for collector and investor loyalties.

As it was, in 1956 Topps became the unchallenged King of the bubblegum card market. Say what you want, but Topps probably earned its position with some great sets in the early 1950s; sets that are still being discovered by collectors and investors today.

"The $6,500 Question,"
the famous 1952 Topps
Mickey Mantle card (#311).

(Copyright Topps Chewing
Gum, Inc.)

The first major Topps set, the famous and fabled 1952 issue, is one that can give anyone a lot of sleepless nights. While Topps had some early ventures into cards before 1952, they are not regarded by many as real sets. But there is no question about the 1952 issue. Nor is there a question that it is an extremely difficult issue to acquire today. With even common players starting at $20 in near mint, and dozens of big names in the $100 to $200 range, this set is out of the price range of many collectors. That does not seem to stop people from spending whatever it takes and stretching their credit as far as they can to complete their collections, or at least grab for a near mint $6,500 Mantle or $1,600 Eddie Mathews.

Is a card like the 1952 Mantle a good investment? That is perilously close to the "$6,500 Question." In a hot Mantle market, it probably is not overpriced. In the Summer of 1988, two low-grade examples of the Mantle were advertised, both under $1,000 (although one of the cards was just barely under that level). Both cards were sold within an hour! Now, if cards graded in the good condition range sell that quickly, then indeed, there have to be people out there willing to pay a lot more for a real nice specimen. Despite that, we are not convinced that the 1952 Mickey Mantle Topps card is an especially good investment from a standpoint of percentages. Let's look at the numbers.

Does this 1957 Topps (#35) rookie card of HOFer Frank Robinson have better profit potential than a '52 Mantle?

(Copyright Topps Chewing Gum, Inc.)

Consider the Mickey Mantle 1952 Topps card in near mint condition at $6,500. Unless you are a good negotiator, to get back your investment with no real profit, the card might have to increase to $10,000 or even more. Compare that to something like a 1956 Luis Aparicio rookie at $50, a 1957 Bill Mazeroski rookie at $12, Don Drysdale at $100, or a Frank Robinson also from that same year at about $125. All of their chances to double in value, meaning some profit to the original buyer, seem far better than Mantle at $6,500, especially when the Mantle cards already have just experienced a big jump in values. That is the problem with any high-priced card. It has to become substantially higher-priced before you usually can make a profit. And, when the card does go so much higher, it will lose a lot of potential buyers along the way.

With all the popularity of sets from 1948 to 1980, you could easily assume that all the potentially good buys have been found and bought. That's not really true. There are a number of underpriced Hall of Famers (HOFers), sleepers who eventually might make Cooperstown, and also a few cards that are probably disaster waiting to happen.

Let's look first at some HOFers who could still go a long way. The Aparicio, Drysdale, and Robinson rookies mentioned above— especially Aparicio—meet our definition of underpriced HOFers. Another who does is Billy Williams, and despite the publicity of his

The 1951 Bowman rookie card (#198) of HOFer Monte Irvin.

recent 1987 induction into Cooperstown, his 1961 rookie card seems very reasonable at around $35. In the 1955 Topps set, the Harmon Killebrew rookie currently at about $150 in near mint still seems to have potential for growth.

Almost without exception, the Bowman rookies such as Berra, Campanella, the 1950 Stengel (not his rookie card, of course, but his first Bowman card), the Robin Roberts, and Monte Irvin cards all seem very reasonable. Can you explain why an Irvin rookie card in near mint condition is only about $30? We can't. His situation is very similar to Satchel Paige; both played for years in the Negro Leagues and did not appear on major league cards until they were well into their pro careers. But the Irvin card is only about $30 and the Bowman "rookie" card of Paige is about $950. Sure, Paige is the bigger name, and the two cards were two years apart being issued, but that huge price difference just makes no sense.

HOFers do not need to be rookie cards to have potential. Paige had only one Topps card, that was in 1953. It is not cheap at $225 in near mint, but if you want a nice Satchel Paige you may have to pay the price. In other cases, the high prices of rookie cards may force many to settle for later year cards which in some respects makes more sense anyway as they have more complete information on the player. Let's assume you can not afford $500

The only major Topps card of HOFer Satchel Paige (spelled "Satchell" on the card) is from the 1953 series (#220).

(Copyright Topps Chewing Gum, Inc.)

for a Clemente rookie. You can still fill your need for a Clemente in near mint for under $20, or under $10 if you don't mind an All Star card. (Virtually all All Star baseball cards are worth considerably less than other regular cards of the same players in the same set.) Clemente is certainly not the only example, similar situations exist for almost every big name in baseball. Their non-rookie cards are often many dollars cheaper, yet more informative than their first cards.

If you think these non-rookies have no investment potential you apparently missed the recent Mickey Mantle craze where there was virtually no such thing as a mint condition Mantle card for under $100. If a player gets hot and his rookie card gets expensive, the situation will carry all the rest of his cards right along, and sometimes those non-rookie cards will do as well or even better than the rookie, increasing by a higher percentage. Don't ever forget the importance of percentages.

As a general rule of thumb, whenever there is a chance to buy mint condition, pre-1980 Hall of Fame inductees for moderate prices, it is probably a wise long-term investment. That's even truer if they are big names and if their cards are pre-1975. Just be extremely fussy about the card's condition and you can not go too far wrong.

A final area that is still being overlooked when it comes to

HOFers are the multi-player cards. For years, the cards with more than one player pictured on them have gotten a bum rap in terms of their prices. Okay, so they're not the same as a single player card, but no one wastes any time quickly buying rookie cards with three or four heads on them. If today's buyers ignored them, you would not have seen such big jumps in prices for the $525 1963 Pete Rose rookie (co-starring Pedro Gonzalez, Ken McMullen, and Al Weis) or the $175 1973 Mike Schmidt rookie (also picturing Ron Cey and John Hilton). What should a card with all HOFers and not three lesser lights be worth? What would a Ruth and Gehrig, or Ruth and Cobb combination card be worth today?

The multi-player card of the current era goes back to Bowman color cards of 1953 where they had a Billy Martin and Phil Rizzuto card, as well as one with Yogi Berra, Hank Bauer, and Mickey Mantle. The following year, Topps countered with the O'Brien twins, Ed and Johnny, and slowly but surely the multi-player card became a fixture in the Topps issues of the late 1950s and into the 1970s. They frequently were used to depict two, three or four rookie prospects at a time.

Before you start grabbing up every multi-player card you can find, let's put this into honest perspective. These cards are not the steal they were a few years ago. They have been discovered, at least to a degree, but they still have potential in many cases, lots of potential in a few, and as little potential as ever in the case of such classics as the 1961 "Power For Ernie" card featuring Ernie Broglio, Daryl Spencer and Bill White.

Actually, that was hardly the worst example, not even from 1961, a year that gave collectors such important moments and cards as "Batter Bafflers" featuring Don Cardwell and Glen Hobbie. These examples point out the first rule of multi-player cards: You should not invest money on cards depicting a lot players who you would not buy if they were depicted individually on cards. Ideally, what you want in a multi-player card are HOFers, especially, the biggest names, like Mantle and Mays who appear together on the fairly expensive 1962 Topps "Manager's Dream" card. Whenever possible, you want only stars. Lesser names pull down values dramatically.

While cards featuring Mantle, such as his pairing with Hank Aaron in the 1958 "World Series Batting Foes," are fairly expen-

A popular example of a HOFer multi-player card is #418 in the 1958 Topps set showing sluggers Mickey Mantle and Hank Aaron.
(Copyright Topps Chewing Gum, Inc.)

sive in top grades, other Aaron multi-player issues seem rather inexpensive, and with lots of room for growth. For instance, there is the 1959 "Fence Busters" showing Aaron with Eddie Mathews, or the 1963 Aaron and Ernie Banks "Power Plus," and the "Tops in the NL" card of 1964 with Aaron and Willie Mays.

Another form of multi-player card worth considering for long term growth are items like league leaders where you have solid Hall of Fame groupings. The 1966 "NL Batting Leaders" card with Hank Aaron, Roberto Clemente, and Willie Mays is priced at about eight dollars in near mint. For five dollars, there is a National League home run leaders card, and they just happen to be Mays, Willie McCovey, and Billy Williams, all three in the Hall of Fame. Pitchers, too, can be interesting, such as the 1967 "National League Pitching Leaders"—Bob Gibson, Sandy Koufax, Juan Marichal, and Gaylord Perry. While you shouldn't expect too much of these cards for a few years, at five dollars or so each it is a better bet than some of the current rookie cards at that price level.

Although you won't get rich quickly, the multi-player cards offer relatively good security. At their current prices there is little downside risk, and if you're patient they probably will do quite nicely as the league leader cards today are where some of the multi-player cards were around 1980 or 1981.

Contrary to popular belief, it is not simply predicting tomorrow's new stars that can create substantial and quick profits. The Hall of Fame at Cooperstown is instant immortality for a player, and an almost equally immediate increase in demand and higher prices for his cards.

In the case of obvious players, the Pete Roses, Rod Carews, and Tom Seavers, it is no great trick to predict they will be in the Hall of Fame, nor is it especially rewarding financially because so many other collectors are making the same predictions. The trick is picking the players like Bobby Doerr, Billy Williams, Ray Dandridge, and others who one day are good players and the next day they are among the game's elite.

Obviously, none of us has the power to predict who may be enshrined next year. What we can do, however, is seek out potential names and determine if their cards, especially their rookie cards, have good potential values. While the potential HOFer may represent a slightly higher financial risk than the guy who is merely waiting five years after retirement for automatic selection, the potential rewards are much higher. So, for those with a little bit of the gambler in you, it's no more risky than buying a few thousand Bo Jackson rookie cards.

From the early part of the 1950s, one rookie we like is Lew Burdette, a pitcher with a lifetime record of 203 wins and 144 losses. Burdette's 1952 Bowman rookie card is a high number, #244, and is valued at about $35 in near mint. A common high-numbered card of that year runs about $20, a Billy Loes rookie is $30 to $35, and the Roy McMillan is also around $30. Now, Loes had a lifetime record of 80-63, and over his career McMillan hit .243. For just a few dollars more, the Burdette rookie looks like a great value and is typical of the sort of potential Hall of Fame rookies you want.

Our favorite potential HOFers from the 1950s are in the 1957 Topps set. With the Brooks and Frank Robinson and the Don Drysdale rookies in there, this set already is loaded, but it still has some excellent rookie card values. Early in the set, #24, is the rookie card of Bill Mazeroski. With Luis Aparicio already in the Hall of Fame, can Mazeroski be far behind? Having talked with plenty of players from that period, author Paul Green has learned that if Mazeroski does not make Cooperstown, a lot of former players will feel an injustice has been done. You can pick up a near mint Mazeroski for probably less than $15; only about twice as much as some common, non-rookie players from that 1957 Topps set. That is a steal.

Around 1986, Green made the public observation that the Tom Lasorda 1954 Topps rookie cards were underpriced because Lasorda probably will make the Hall of Fame. Apparently many people also are making that observation because the card now is around $100 in near mint and really not underpriced anymore. Whitey "the White Rat" Herzog is also going to be a very hard guy to keep out of Cooperstown. His 1957 Topps rookie card, #29, seems to be an absolute bargain at its current price level of around $12. It may take a few years to take off, but we are convinced that it is a good, if not great deal, at around $12 to $15 in near mint condition.

There are plenty of such rookie cards out there for not much more than some youngsters spend each time they buy an armload of current wax packs. The sleepers for eventual Hall of Fame recognition are numerous. If you're still not convinced, here are more examples. In the 1958 Topps set there's the #420 Vada Pinson rookie for about $7. Pinson had 2,757 hits and a lifetime .286 average. Is he going to be kept out of Cooperstown forever? Is it worth the risk of a few dollars on the belief that he'll eventually get in? Is it true some players spit a lot? At least two of the last three questions can be answered, "Yes."

Need more examples? (Another, "Yes," please.) Take George Anderson, #338, in the 1959 Topps set. Okay, so Anderson only hit .218 for Philadelphia that year. So, he made up for it beginning in 1970 when he took over the helm of the Cincinnati Reds. Since that time his clubs have played in and won more games in the League Championship series for a better winning percentage than any other manager can boast. He also has the third best winning percentage in history in the World Series. Can George "Sparky" Anderson be kept out of the Hall of Fame? We don't think so. More important than what we think, do you think that the current price of $9 or $10 for a 1959 George Anderson rookie card is likely to go to $18 or $20 faster than the currently $450 Tom Seaver rookie card will double to $900? Even though the Seaver card is glamorous, the Anderson card looks like a better value.

You can go up and down the lists, year after year, finding

*A potential HOFer, Sparky
Anderson, on his 1959
Topps rookie card (#338).*
(Copyright Topps Chewing
Gum, Inc.)

rookie cards like Pinson, Anderson, Mazeroski, and Herzog, cards
of people who currently are only a few dollars more than a card
from the same set of some player whose only future role at
Cooperstown might be taking tickets at the front door. The possibilities are numerous, and as long as you avoid the financially fatal
tendency of most fans to evaluate the players only with their
hearts, you probably can find there are plenty of sleepers available
no matter what your budget.

Throughout your examination of cards from 1948 to 1980, as
with any other era, your emphasis should be on value and the potential for the card to double in price over a period of years, not
leaving you with serious financial losses. Being offered a Pete Rose
rookie card at $525 or a Jim Rice rookie at $32 may represent
good prices today, but are the cards good values for the future?
Can you imagine the Rose at $900 or the Rice at $70? That is the
real question when it comes to investment, for they are the minimum levels you'll be likely to need simply to make a very modest
profit; otherwise, just leave your money in the bank, a certificate of
deposit, or a savings bond.

It is hard to dispute the notion that while cards from the 1948
to 1980 era are extremely popular, there are bigger and quicker
dollars to be made from more recent rookie cards. Even so, there
are some potentially excellent investments in cards before 1980,

and the liquidity of these cards—the speed at which they can be turned into cash with a sale—is much better than you'll find with some rookie who managed only a .265 average. At worst, your investment in the cards of 1948 to 1980 might start you on the road to a real collection from that period, and you could do a lot worse than assemble a top grade collection of some of the big names of post-World War II baseball. You, too, will learn to cherish the names of Willie, Mickey, the Duke, Stan the Man, and Ted Williams. It was a golden era that can mean future golden memories and probably a few dollars profit.

Rookie Fever

Why the fever can be financially fatal in small doses or megalots.

In baseball card investing, Rookie Fever is contagious. The symptoms are sudden outbreaks of desire to purchase, at almost any price, cards of rookie players. The fever can quickly overpower your senses, causing delusions of instant wealth while actually sapping both the strength of your collecting spirit and wallet. In acute cases, Rookie Fever can be financially fatal.

Recent baseball seasons have displayed all the signs of unprecedented epidemics of otherwise sound-minded collectors feverishly trying to obtain large quantities of cards depicting each of the year's hottest rookies. Fever victims hallucinate that the value of those cards will perpetually increase in direct proportion to the players' ever-increasing totals of HRs, and RBIs, or, in the case of rookie pitchers, their ever-decreasing ERAs.

The only known cure for these hot flashes is a large dose of cold reality.

For example, by mid-March 1988, the recently-released baseball cards (Fleer #137) of Mets' shortstop prospect Gregg Jefferies were briskly selling for up to five dollars each in the New York area, and close to that elsewhere. These same cards were available wrapped with 14 others in familiar wax packages sold at hobby shops and corner stores for 50 cents or a buck for an entire pack. But Rookie Fever quickly elevated Jefferies' individual cards from two dollars each in January 1988 to a retail value of five dollars two weeks before opening day.

Sure, he batted .333 during spring training, and had been named Minor League Player of the Year the two previous seasons. Sure, he looked like a hot prospect. But five dollars for the current card of a 20 year old who had played in only six regular season major league games?

"I think it is absolutely ludicrous! It's ridiculous," exclaimed well-known and outspoken card dealer Alan Rosen, Montvale, New Jersey. "You could buy a Bob Gibson, Juan Marichal, or a Willy Stargell (non-rookie) card for two, three, or four dollars each."

On Mar. 23, 1988, Gregg Jefferies was sent back to the minors. The value of his baseball cards apparently reaching high tide as he reported to Tidewater of the Triple A International League.

That same day, the large volume dealer-to-dealer trading of his 1988 cards stopped almost as quickly as beer sales at the end of a game. The dealers, collectors, and speculators were suddenly unwilling to buy and sell at the five dollar level, hoping Jefferies would be quickly called back to the majors; otherwise his card price would surely come crashing down. Just like the infamous die-hard Cubs' fans who never give up hope, serious buyers of the Jefferies cards have lots of faith.

"Knowledgeable people were buying the cards because they knew it is going to go higher," said dealer Brent Lee, a rookie card specialist from Anaheim, California. He made the comment five full months before Jefferies was brought back up to the majors to play third base in late August, and in his first two games again in a Mets uniform went five-for-nine including a double, a triple, and his first major league home run!

"Other knowledgeable people who bought the Jefferies' cards at the start of 1988 are refusing to sell them because they also know it will go higher in value. They've done their baseball research and believe that Jefferies could be a much better investment than the lesser rookies whose chances in the majors might be questionable. Someone like Sam Horn might be a better investment rookie card gamble than Gary Thurman," he advised.

The Jefferies and Horn cards are not the only ones that soared in the spring of 1988. Those picturing rookies Ellis Burks, Mark Grace, and Matt Nokes also sold for about a dollar each or more before opening day because of speculation the players eventually will be stars in the major leagues. Prices of 50 cents each or more were asked for cards of Shawn Abner, Roberto Alomar, Todd Benzinger, Geronimo Berroa, Jay Buhner, Ken Caminiti, Rob Ducey, Al Leiter, Jack McDowell, Billy Ripken, Todd Stottlemyre, Jeff Treadway, Gary Thurman, and Gerald Young.

Yet, for less than 50 cents each you could buy the 1988 cards of well-established players such as George Brett, Roger Clemens, Tony Gwynn, Dale Murphy, Kirby Puckett, Nolan Ryan, and Darryl Strawberry.

Jeff Fritsch, whose Stevens Point, Wisconsin, baseball card company has been a family-run business for four decades, believes most rookies' cards are grossly overpriced. "It's nuts. I don't understand how it possibly can be like this, but this is the way the hobby is going. It doesn't make any sense."

The Rookie Fever epidemic started around 1982 and has infected all but a few collectors in the marketplace. It begins to quickly spread each January when the major card companies (Donruss, Fleer, Topps, and now Score) release their first sets of the new year. By spring training the mania contaminates the collecting habits of several million Americans who eagerly speculate on which fresh faces of the new season will be the next Don Mattingly, Wally Joyner, Brooks Robinson, or Willy Mays. And, they want to figure it out before other card buyers pump up the prices of those future stars' rookie cards.

"Since 1982, it is harder to fool other dealers and get the 'hidden' rookies' cards cheaply," admitted Skokie, Illinois, dealer Brian Sawada. "Everyone now can read about the hot prospects in *USA Today, Baseball Digest,* and everywhere else."

Sawada believes that news media attention is an important factor in the price of a player's cards, rookie or veteran. "If a player is with a team located in a media center like New York, Chicago, or Los Angeles he gets more attention. Tim Raines and Tony Gwynn cards are undervalued because they play in Montreal and San

Diego. If George Bell gets traded to New York his cards will go up; he can't hide in Toronto forever."

Soon after first being released in 1984, the Donruss rookie cards (#248) of Yankees first baseman Mattingly could be purchased for perhaps $2.50. Today, those same cards sell for $65 each. Mattingly not only hit six grand slams in the 1987 season, he has the luck of playing in *the* media center, New York City, and on a team owned by the never-publicity-shy George Steinbrenner.

Rookie cards of former superstar players also have been jumping in value. For example, in 1987, mint condition specimens of the Topps 1957 card (#328) of Baltimore's Hall of Fame third baseman Brooks Robinson were valued at about $200. Now, they command $500 and up. (Virtually all high-quality 1950s Topps cards have significantly appreciated in value the past year, but those of the stars have done even better.) Robinson earned his stature with 23 years in the major leagues, not pre-season speculation.

"It's going to be tough for Gregg Jefferies to perform as well as his card has performed," predicted dealer Jim Carr, Pehlam, New Hampshire, who begins each baseball season by purchasing as many as 20,000 cards for each of a dozen or more rookie prospects. "It is a way of expressing how you feel about a particular player," he explained.

Carr has been making those kinds of costly financial expressions since 1982, and not just for current rookie cards.

"I also like to buy large quantities of the last cards issued for players such as Nolan Ryan and Reggie Jackson. Everyone wants a rookie card of someone like a Wade Boggs, a card that has absolutely no information on the back (about a star's lengthy, successful career). But you can buy Rod Carew's last year in the majors with all the information, all his batting statistics, and it is the cheapest card that exists for this player. You can buy it for maybe ten cents. Yet, it has all his stats on it, that he won seven batting titles, what he batted each year, and it is so much more interesting than his rookie card.

"I've taken guys I'm basically sure will be in the Hall of Fame and bought 10,000 or 20,000 of their cards. Nolan Ryan, Reggie Jackson, Rod Carew, Tom Seaver, and others we've watched playing for 10 or 15 years. They're definitely going to be in the Hall of Fame, but you can buy their last years' cards for a dime each. That seems like an excellent value," Carr suggested.

"I think that 10 or 20 years from now, when the kids of today are 30 or 40 years old and can afford to spend some money on cards, these are probably the cards they're going to want."

Dealer Rosen, whose hobby nickname, "Mr. Mint," could easily apply to either his well-known zeal for high-quality condition cards or being able to afford his 1988 buying binge that totaled more than $2 million in baseball card purchases, agrees with Carr about the lopsided pricing.

For example, the much-publicized 1952 first Topps card of Mickey Mantle is being offered for as much as $8,000 to $10,000 in pristine condition, while "a Topps 1969 Mantle is a $150 card and you can't even fit all of his stats on the back of it," Rosen pointed out.

"The Tom Seaver rookie card (1967 Topps #581) is about $500 in mint, but his last cards from last year are only a nickel each, and they have all of his wins listed on them.

"Warren Spahn, one of the greatest pitchers who ever pitched, has a 1948 Bowman card (#18) that goes for spit (only about $100). His last regular card, issued when he was a coach with the Mets in 1965 and listing all of his 350 or so wins, is worth just eight dollars. And, a Gregg Jefferies card is worth five dollars? It just doesn't make any sense to me. It's crazy."

Jefferies went back to the major league in late August 1988 and picked up where speculators thought he would. In the last weeks of the regular season he batted .321 with six home runs. His cards jumped to eight dollars each!

For every potential Mantle, Mays, and Mattingly, there are dozens of rookies whose stars quickly fell, or never rose much above the horizon.

Consider the plunging values of cards depicting former Detroit pitcher Mark "The Bird" Fidrych and Cleveland outfielder Joe Charboneau. Fidrych was American League Rookie of the Year in 1976, Charboneau received that honor in 1980. The Bird's 1977 rookie cards (Topps #265) quickly flew to several dollars each, the same for Charboneau's 1981 cards (Topps #13 and Donruss #82).

The values for the cards of Mark Fidrych, Joe Charboneau, and Ron Kittle all fell as their on-field stats slid.

(Copyright Topps Chewing Gum, Inc.)

But when their on-field abilities took a dive, so did the values. You can buy all the rookie Fidrych and Charboneau cards you want today for only about 25 cents each—or less. And, the dealer will be grateful for helping him clear his shelves.

Just a few seasons ago, Chicago fans eagerly were paying three dollars apiece for the 1983 cards (Fleer #241 and Topps #X-55) of White Sox home run slugger and Rookie of the Year, Ron Kittle. When his bat cooled the cards turned to ice. Kittle's moves to the Yankees, the Indians, and then back to the Sox have not thawed the price. His rookie cards also are a shelf-clearing 25 cents each.

The value of a rookie player's baseball cards is affected by what he does in the minor leagues and in spring training. Later, the price depends on what he does on the field in the majors, and even what he does long after hanging up his spikes. See following chart.

Rookies of the Year (Selected)

	Bob Horner #589 1979T	Rick Sutcliffe #544 1980T
1981	$3.00	.03
1982	3.15	.03
1983	3.50	.05
1984	4.00	.05
1985	2.50	2.50
1986	2.50	2.25
1987	4.50	1.50
1988	3.00	3.00

Dwight Gooden	1984 #82	1984TT #42	1985D #190
1985	1.75	4.25	2.50
1986	5.50	35.00	7.00
1987	7.00	40.00	10.00
1988	70.00	35.00	10.00

Joe Charboneau	1981F #397	1981T #13
1982	.25	.25
1983	.04	.04
1984	.04	.04
1985	.04	.04
1986	.04	.05
1987	.05	.07
1988	.05	.07

Ron Kittle	1983 TT #55	1984D #244	1983F #241
1984	2.75		2.75
1985	3.00	.25	2.50
1986	2.00	.25	1.00
1987	1.00	.40	1.00
1988	.60	.30	.70

Early in 1987, speculation about his potential in the majors already had boosted Mark McGwire's 1985 rookie card (Topps #401) to about a dollar, and it steadily increased. Then, during the national sports collectors' convention in San Francisco in the summer of 1987, the card jumped in value five dollars in one day because of McGwire's home run marathon over a July weekend. The price has continued to climb along with his list of accomplishments.

"Now is a good time to buy some of the 1987 cards of players like Will Clark and Wally Joyner," dealer Lee believes. "Or, a great time to sell cards like McGwire and Mike Greenwell that went up so much they make up for the 80 percent of the others that did not go up, or went down in value."

Rosen is still not convinced: "You can buy the 1973 Willie Mays Topps card for only about $13, yet a McGwire rookie card now sells for $20. That's unbelievable.

"Rookie cards can be summed up as: 'What have you done for me lately.' You strike out, the card goes down; you hit a home run, the card goes up in value," Rosen said.

"Splashy statistics, a 30 game winner or 300 strike-outs, get attention," Lee emphasized. "A consistent player, like a pitcher who wins 18 games a year for ten years in a row, may not be recognized (by baseball card buyers)."

Even when a player is doing well on the playing field, his off-field activities can significantly affect the value of his cards. Within two years of their release, Dwight Gooden's rookie 1984 Fleer cards (#U-43) shot to $120 each. *Playboy* magazine even praised them as one of the best financial investments of the year. Although the value teetered a bit with Gooden's less-than-spectacular 1986 World Series performance, the plunge began a few months later when he and Florida police had a close encounter of the unpleasant kind.

When news reports of Gooden's cocaine problems became an

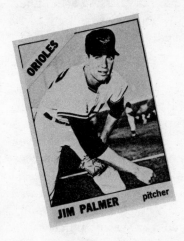

The 1966 Topps rookie
card (#126) of super star
Jim Palmer whose so-so
first year in the majors in
1965 probably would not
have caused rookie fever
today.

(Copyright Topps Chewing
Gum, Inc.)

everyday story, some dealers were happy to sell his rookie card for
only $30. It now is listed at about $65.

What about potential Hall of Fame players who just do not
have a fabulous first year? Phillies star Mike Schmidt only batted
.196 in his 1973 rookie year. He wondered if he would have a second season in the majors! Cy Young award winning pitcher Jim
Palmer had a so-so rookie season with Baltimore in 1965 when he
was 5-4 with an ERA of 3.72. Their first cards (1973 Topps #615
and 1966 Topps #126) are priced today at about $200 and $50,
but if they started as rookies this season with those kinds of playing
statistics few collectors would be paying any premium for their
cards.

Occasionally, a player's off-field performances outshine his
otherwise ordinary on-field abilities. An excellent example cited in
another chapter of this book is Bob Uecker, star of the "Mr. Belvedere" television series, star of beer commercials, star Brewers play-
by-play broadcaster, and, oh yes, former catcher. By his own
admission his playing career was "good field, no hit," but his 1962
Topps rookie card (#594) has passed the $100 mark in mint condi-
tion compared to $35 just a year earlier. The price has jumped be-
cause of Uecker's status as a media personality, not the stats of his
professional baseball career.

Even with solid research and educated guessing about future superstars, the experts can be wrong. Superbly successful dealer Rosen admitted: "Every time I've dived into the rookie cards, I have not been successful.

"In 1982, Dave Righetti started out four and zero. I really went in big, buying 20,000 of his cards for sixty cents each. A month later, he was four and four, and then sent back to the minor leagues. Bret Saberhagen has been up and down like a yo-yo. He had one great year and his card went to four dollars. The next year you couldn't get a dollar for it. Then, the first part of the next year he starts out with nine wins and the card shoots back to five dollars. The second half of the year he fell apart and the card went back down to a dollar again."

Despite his carefully considered pre-season purchases of more than 100,000 rookie cards, dealer Carr revealed: "Unfortunately, I did not buy any Gregg Jefferies or GaryThurman cards."

Not all heated cases of Rookie Fever are easily cured even with a large dose of cold reality, but there is a simple treatment that is effective with all collectors. You take one of everything.

"My opinion of collecting cards is to buy sets," suggested dealer Fritsch. "If you buy an entire set you've got all the players. If particular players do well, you've got them; if they bomb, you've still got the other cards.

Collecting fads are cyclical, they tend to come and go as marketplace trends change every decade or so. As a colorful collectible, rookie baseball cards surely will remain an alluring part of the hobby. As a speculative investment, they could be a financially fatal attraction.

But rookie cards are exciting as well as frantic and high-risk. There can be enormous profits and/or staggering losses, all in a few months.

Have you won a lottery lately? Have you let it all "ride" on the roulette wheel or craps table in Las Vegas—then lost? You can come perilously close to these sensations with the financial speculation of rookie card fever, and you don't need a license to do it. Some might even suggest you don't need brains, either, but we'll get to that later. All you need to do is fasten your seat belt and loosen your wallet.

The rookie card market used to be rather innocent. You

bought a pack of cards for five cents and maybe you got a Mantle. That made it a good pack, unless you happened to be rooting for the Dodgers, in which case it was suddenly a bad pack. You could always trade that Mantle for your favorite player at the time, like Clem Labine, which made it a good pack after all; but a terrible investment even if you happened to keep your cards in nice condition and your mother never threw them away.

In some ways it is still innocent today. You spend your 40 cents or whatever the pack costs, and you hope you get a Mark McGwire rookie or something similar. If you're lucky you either keep that card or some smiling dealer will pay you a few dollars for it. Not bad for 18 seconds of work, and you still have more than a dozen other cards from the pack—along with a stick of gum, a puzzle piece, or some other premium.

That's rookie card fever in a pure form. Of course, now computerized systems can determine just what cards you'll probably find inside a cellophane-wrapped package (cello pack) just by peeking at the visible top and bottom cards, and then you can determine in advance if you'll make or lose money if you buy that particular pack. And, there are those who say, "If I can make $1.60 profit on one McGwire card, why not have them by the thousands?"

Therein lie the seeds of the megalot market. It's not a formal place like the New York Stock Exchange. Rather, it's a lot of people on the telephones, teletype circuits, and other modern marvels of communications buying and selling baseball cards. It sounds innocent so far, right? Where it becomes sinister to some is that they're not buying and selling the stray Lou Gehrig or Yogi Berra card. No, they're dealing in 10,000 Wally Joyners, or 5,000 Mike Greenwells. That is the megalot market, a place for the financially well-endowed and the strong of heart and nerve.

To the average collector, the megalot market is a strange and bizarre place, a concept out of science fiction. The collector buys a set and is content with one card of each player. The big rookie card buyer wants comparatively few different cards, but instead wants 1,000 or 10,000 of the same specific players. They want to multiply the profits and magnify the losses in a glorious rush of activity where you win or lose based on your ability to pick prospects, buy them right, sell them right, and all with that little element of chance (how the player actually performs on the field and off) thrown in to keep things interesting. Perhaps a bottle of Pepto Bismol is nearby, too.

In some respects, the rookie card market is like the market in penny stocks. Bought and sold like real stocks, the penny stocks offer the attraction of very low prices, a few dollars or even a few cents per share. The penny stocks allow even the person of average means to act like a corporate giant, moving thousands of shares on a whim. It's almost a pleasant fantasy, except the money being used is real. If your gold mine turns out to be full of bats (the flying kind) and no gold, your $10,000 worth of the venture can become nearly worthless in an instant. If, however, it turns out to be the next great gold mine, you can leave the penny stocks behind and start playing with the Blue Chips and other major companies with your huge, new profits.

The penny stock is to a share of IBM what a 1989 rookie card is to a 1933 Goudey Babe Ruth card. Lower priced, less prestigious and far more volatile in price. They are pieces of paper that represent relatively cheap thrills compared to the other investments of their type.

Cheap, but dangerous paper, and paper with unique problems. That is especially true with the rookie card. While it may be similar to the penny stock, remember no gold mine ever threw out its arm in April or had a drug problem in July. And as mentioned before, storing a penny stock does not require a spare room, but 10,000 Jose Canseco cards probably will. And, when you want to sell your shares of stock, you can simply call a stock broker. When you want to sell those 3,000 John Kruk rookies in your attic you haul them to a card show or local dealer and keep your fingers crossed. If they're not John Kruks, but rather a good rookie gone bad, you need not bother with the show or the neighborhood dealer because those cards are almost certainly yours to keep with little or no prospect of getting them out of your house without taking a financial beating. Somebody might purchase a Joe Charboneau card to complete a set, but nobody wants 100 of them, or 1,000, or heaven forbid, 10,000. Those numbers are no laughing matter as the joke turns cruel. Nothing is as worthless as the star who never was; like an injured player, everyone turns their back and walks away because the bad luck might spread, and so might the financial disaster.

Before you buy your first modern rookie card it is important to understand the market. A decade ago virtually no one even considered the notion of buying 10, 100, or 1,000 cards of the same player unless it was for a dealer's stock. Even then, buying so many current cards of the same freshmen players would have been considered a bit unusual.

The rookie card market is growing by leaps and bounds, but even so, it is still a young market and the rules could change quickly and dramatically. At present, there are plenty of willing buyers or traders if the quantity of cards involved is small. One 1985 McGwire card would not be difficult to sell. Even in amounts of 5 to 25, it has not been terribly hard to find buyers for the currently "hot" rookie prospects. The problem faced by investors is when they move from the category of casual investor to the mega-lot speculator. The more people in that market, the greater the liquidity of the right cards. While there may be thousands of buyers for a single card, there may only be a half dozen potential buyers for a thousand copies of that same card.

The reasons are simple. While modern rookie cards may only cost a dime apiece, those dimes can add up quickly. It is not hard even at a dime each to end up with hundreds or thousands of dollars in rookie cards, cards you know are not rare as they are being produced in the hundreds of millions, perhaps even billions. Moreover, they do not represent a collection. Thousands of Danny Tartabull cards are almost menacing to a collector or small store owner. Even if they think Tartabull is the greatest player since Ruth, they can't imagine what they would do with 5,000 of his cards.

Not only do all those cards represent a lot of money being tied up, it is volatile money, something perilously close to a ticking time bomb waiting for the dreaded moment when the player is injured, goes into a slump, or is found to have a drug problem. You can't control such things, but when it is your money they are easy to imagine, and sometimes they actually do happen. Most people won't sleep well at night with 10,000 Greg Swindell rookies in their closet.

And even if you can sleep at night with your 10,000 David Cones, to cash in on your investment you need to find someone else who can sleep after buying them from you, presumably at a higher price than you originally paid. That may not be easy. The modern rookie baseball card market currently is not a very liquid market for the megalot transaction. You can buy 5,000 cards easily enough at retail prices, but selling them can take a lot of time and effort, and it can knock down your eventual price from the level you expected to receive. There is not much of a "secondary" market for megalot quantities, just as there is not much of a secondary market for many special cards, such as the sets produced for retail store chains (see chapter 9).

A second and also very important aspect of the rookie card market is that the more something costs, the harder people resist paying the price. For example, in 1987 some Eric Davis rookie cards dramatically took off. Helped by national publicity, the cards (1985 Donruss #325) soared from four dollars each through the $10 level and beyond. For a time, $30 or even $40 did not seem out of the question. But then, almost as suddenly as it started, those $25 Eric Davis cards just stopped going up. Essentially, the same thing happened with Mark McGwire. Early in the 1987 season, his Topps card (#366) of that year might have been overpriced at 50 cents each. Then he started hitting home runs at a potentially record-breaking pace and the card moved along with his soaring statistics. By July of that year you could walk the floor of any card show and find McGwire rookies for two dollars, then $2.50 and even up to $10 each. But somewhere around that level, the home runs became less frequent, and the card dropped back in price. McGwire's price boom was over as people discovered he was indeed human, and they also discovered Kevin Seitzer and Benito Santiago. A similar situation occurred in 1988 with the Chicago Cubs' Mark Grace and the Cincinnati Reds' Chris Sabo.

Price resistance seems to come quickly with modern rookie cards. They have their month or two in the spotlight, and then suddenly the explosion is over. Sales continue, of course, but generally at a slower pace and often times at lower prices. The market also seems to have a somewhat cyclical nature. The new cards make their first appearance while the snow is still on the ground in many locations. Based on an assortment of factors (mostly what the market will bear), general prices are established and the rookie card market moves into a new year. Injuries, cuts from the roster, and other natural disasters take their toll, and some of the top-rated rookies start falling by the wayside as early as the end of spring training—including otherwise excellent players, like Gregg Jefferies.

By the end of spring training, some other cards are starting to gain attention, a situation that continues for the first half of the season. During these early summer months the demand begins peaking for some rookies who got off to a good start, and demand begins waning for other players who are still available for purchase but who are almost totally unsalable at wholesale levels.

By the last half of the major league schedule the market is starting to clearly reflect the rookies' seasons. Usually new names are popping up, names like Santiago, Bonilla, and Aldrete in recent years. In many instances, the early hot names have peaked, while the new names will draw attention for a few months before the next year's cards begin to appear in the marketplace. At that point, the cards of the previous year—the McGwires and the others—are almost old news. Unless they have a major change in their fate on the field they may become relatively quiet only to be rediscovered at a later time.

There are definite likes and dislikes in the rookie marketplace. Buyers want spectacular, crowd-pleasing performances. The power-hitting rookie, such as Mark McGwire, is the most desirable. The high average hitter ranks a fairly close second. Starting pitchers and defensive specialists rank well behind these others, and relief pitchers have little real market value at present.

While prices are influenced primarily by what a player does on the field, there are other factors. Not only are the ballplayers' skills and characteristics important, but things like the team they're affiliated with also factor in. Why is a team so important? Almost everyone in New England roots for the Boston Red Sox. That means there is a large market for Red Sox cards there, especially Red Sox rookies. Demand in New York for any new Mets or Yankees players tends to border on the insane, a scramble to be the first on your block to obtain the first cards. But, as we mentioned earlier in this chapter, in the New York area the Jefferies cards shot up to five dollars each in early 1988 before it was learned he did not make the team. At the same time, players laboring in "distant outposts" of major league baseball, like Seattle, receive far less national media attention—and therefore, far less interest in the rookie card market. It's not just Seattle, either. Look at Toronto, San Diego, Montreal and a few others and you'll quickly find that if you compare the statistics of a Montreal rookie and a young player from New York, the Expo card will be cheaper, often quite a bit cheaper, even if the two players' stats are comparable. Eventually, a Hall of Fame candidate from Montreal will be discovered, but it will take longer and his card's price climb will be less spectacular than someone similarly gifted but wearing Yankee pinstripes.

Another important characteristic of the rookie card market is that by and large it is a Topps-based market. There are a few exceptions, but generally the people who want to buy 10,000 Joey Meyer rookie cards often can not easily get the quantities of Donruss, Fleer or Score cards needed to sustain the market. That also explains why the large lot (megalot) rookie card market is restricted almost totally to cards produced since 1985. There simply are not 5,000 Cal Ripken or George Bell 1982 rookie cards regularly available at one time from any dealer. Since you can not sell what you can not buy in sufficient quantities, you either must deal in smaller lots, or not at all.

Even with current rookie cards, adequate supplies are sometimes a problem. In 1987, Kevin Seitzer of Kansas City and Benito Santiago of San Diego were on their way to impressive rookie seasons. With no Topps rookie cards of either during most of the year, the market was frustrated. Paying a little extra for a Fleer rookie card because it is tough to find may be okay for the collector or casual investor, but if you're buying them by the hundreds or thousands then an extra quarter here and an extra dime there can turn into a lot of dollars very quickly—dollars that may be very difficult to recoup at liquidation time. Until there are adequate supplies of other card brands available, the major activities in modern rookie cards will remain a Topps-based market.

There are actually some advantages to Topps for those interested in large lots. There is a moderating factor at work. In early 1988, cards like those of Jefferies were going crazy while he was going to Tidewater. With no Topps cards available there were very few substantial losses for investors. It was difficult to locate large quantities of the Jefferies' Fleer and Donruss cards. The flip side is the 1988 Grace card. Although he was sent down to the minors for a while, he returned to the Cubs and began producing the kinds of numbers that get people talking about possible Rookie of the Year awards. Those Grace cards, purchased at lower prices early in the season when he was not making headlines, probably will do well, assuming Grace himself continues to do well, too.

The delay in waiting to obtain Topps cards can not be defined as either good or bad. At the present time, it appears to be about neutral in terms of investors' bank balances. Not buying Santiago or Seitzer in 1987 seems to be wise in terms of Santiago, and less so in terms of Seitzer, but even there, his 1988 Topps card opened the year at fairly modest levels and should do very well over the years if he continues to hit at a clip of .300 a season for the next 15 years.

Another very important factor for the rookie card, especially the megalot quantity, is that price and the player's on-the-field performance are directly related. This might seem obvious, but the speed with which it takes place in the marketplace is not reflected in any price guide. That flurry, mentioned earlier, of McGwire home runs during the weekend of the 1987 National Sports Collectors Convention in San Francisco saw his cards shoot up in price immediately, days if not weeks before those price increases would be reflected in price guides and advertisements.

It doesn't just happen when a player is doing well. Dwight Gooden's drug problems caused an immediate softening of demand and price for his cards. Greg Swindell's 1987 card had become virtually unsalable in large quantities long before price guides and advertisements reflected lower prices. Bo Jackson's strikeouts in 1987 began taking a terrible toll on both the demand and the value of his rookie cards in the megalot market long before he announced he planned to join the Los Angeles Raiders and again play football, an announcement that further forced down price levels. (On Friday, Apr. 3, 1987, just as the major league baseball season was getting underway, co-author of this book, Donn Pearlman, appeared on the NBC-TV program, "Today," to promote his earlier book, *Collecting Baseball Cards*. Interviewer Bryant Gumble held up a 1986 Bo Jackson rookie baseball card and asked how high its value would go if Jackson only played one or two successful baseball seasons, then quit to become an outstanding professional football player. Pearlman emphasized that under those circumstances Jackson's *football* cards could become valuable, not his baseball cards. Gumble seemed skeptical at the time, but the marketplace indicates Pearlman's prediction is much closer to reality.)

Which all leads to the first and most critical rule of rookie card investing: If you're going to invest in rookies, you had better study rookies like your financial future depends on it, for it very may well.

Let's assume you are indeed going to invest in modern rookie cards. What follows is a bit of general advice on how to do it, and hopefully, how to enjoy and prosper from the experience. The first rule you must remember, in addition to carefully studying young players, is that you are going to have some winners and some losers. If you pick nothing but winners, you should be working in the front office of the Atlanta Braves or touring the country as a scout for the White Sox, not wasting your special talents investing in rookie baseball cards. Accept the fact that there will be losers, probably more of them than long-term winners.

Before buying your first rookie cards you better also understand what types of cards to purchase, and that can get rather confusing. What is not confusing is that you only want mint condition cards. Well-centered, clean cards, not ones that would be super except for this little problem or that little flaw. Coming right from the pack is no longer good enough because some cards right from the pack are off-center, have chewing gum stains, ink streaks, or other problems. Leave those problem cards for someone else. If they're a problem today, you can bet they'll be an even bigger problem tomorrow for the person to whom you're trying to sell them.

The next question is a big one: "Which rookie cards should you purchase?" That may seem a little odd after you've done your homework, but consider Jim Presley who appeared in regular Fleer and Donruss sets in 1985 (#500 and #240) and the Topps traded set (#T-92) issued late that year, but not in the regular Topps set of 1985. That initial regular Topps set appearance had to wait until 1986 (#598). One definition of a rookie card is that it is a true rookie card whether it is issued in a regular set at the beginning of the year, or in a year-end set (traded, extended, updated, or whatever phrase the card companies may use). Yet, another definition holds that rookie cards must be available in a regularly-issued, nationally-distributed set and that a card from any other Traded, Updated, Rookies, Highlights, or similar set not available to the general public is not a true *rookie* card, although it still may be considered the player's *first* card. Of course, there also is the confusion over McGwire's 1985 Topps card (#401) showing him as a member of the 1984 U.S. Olympic Baseball Team and the "regular" cards issued in 1987 by Donruss (#46 and Rookies #1) and Fleer (#U-76).

Frankly, this confusion over a player's real rookie card is a wonderful way for the card companies to sell more cards and for the dealers to sell more card sets. The debate over when a rookie card really is a rookie card has continued for years without resolution. In 1986, there was a classic example with the Jose Canseco card (#T-20) distributed in the Topps traded set at the end of the year. That card currently sells for around seven dollars. He had rookie cards in the regular Donruss and Fleer sets (#39 and #649) that sell for around $50 and $30 respectively. His first regular issue Topps card was 1987 (#620) and it now lists at around $3. If you consider that any Jose Canseco card cost only about a few cents initially, then they have all done well. While all the 1986 cards might be more desirable, the buyer who wants 1,000 Cansecos probably will purchase 1987 Topps cards as they are the only ones available in adequate quantities. While that may seem like a handicap, the 1987's, like others in the past, will still rise and fall with his fortunes, just less dramatically perhaps than the 1986 issue.

The situation is not unique to Topps. In any given year, a company will miss a big name rookie, eventually picking him up in their year-end set, and causing more confusion. The major card companies carefully study rookie prospects during the off-season, but still, there are so many potential rookies, and just so many can be selected for the regular sets distributed at the beginning of each year, months before spring training camps even open. If you want more than a few hundred cards of a given rookie, finding adequate numbers in the End of Year, Traded, Updated, or whatever sets is likely to be a big problem. Consequently, the bulk of the huge card purchases still are regular-issue Topps, and although another company or two eventually may produce enough cards to become a staple of that market, for the present, if you want 3,000 cards of one player you're almost certainly talking about his regular issue Topps cards.

The next issue is how to find the rookie cards where you want to place your money. It is not terribly hard to determine that names like Dwight Gooden, Wade Boggs, Jose Canseco, Mark McGwire, Don Mattingly, and a host of others are good rookie cards. You need only look at a price guide and some recent major league statistics to see that. Whether such names have any real upward potential is another matter entirely. Despite an excellent 1987 season, Don Mattingly rookie cards remained the same price or actually declined a little during 1988, and for most rookies since 1980, prospects for future major price climbs would seem marginal at best given their current values.

Another rule to remember: If you really expect or hope to make money in recent rookie cards you will make it in "sleepers," and most often in the prospective player you correctly identified when his card was purchased for a dime and you sold it for a couple of dollars.

Identifying the future star while he is still in the minor leagues does not involve alchemy or astrology, it involves studying, reading, and even getting out whenever possible to check out a prospect or two yourself. The people who regularly trade in megalots do these things, and whether you're buying one card or 10,000 it helps to know what and who you're buying. Your goal in rookie card buying is not to buy the card everyone else is purchasing, but rather to buy it *before* they want to purchase it. To do that you must start at the minor league or college level because that is where the stars of tomorrow are playing today.

The first key to identifying a prospect is reading. If you do not have a subscription to *Baseball America* which offers the most complete coverage of minor league baseball available today, you are not ready to buy rookie cards as an investment. More than any other publication, this one enables you to follow a prospect from his college or first professional appearance right up to the majors. In addition, during the season and all winter you'll need to read whatever other information you can about baseball both on the major and minor league levels. It also helps to listen to sports pro-

One of the hottest 1988 Fleer cards, rookie Gregg Jefferies of the New York Mets (#137).

grams where scouts, general managers, and others discuss their team and the opposition. There are a wide range of publications that can help. The *Sporting News* has long been something close to the Bible on baseball. *Baseball Digest, Sports Illustrated,* a new publication called *Baseball Today,* and a host of others also provide excellent coverage.

You are looking for the player who has excellent minor league credentials (and perhaps end-of-the season major league experience because he was briefly brought up to the majors for a few weeks). You also want someone who has a future role with a major league club. It's an important consideration, but one that is too often forgotten.

Let's take a couple of examples of promising players with high rookie card prices. In 1987, when Dave Magadan was brought up by the New York Mets, his rookie cards were an instant hit because, after all, Magadan could hit, and do so with the best of them. Just like Gregg Jefferies in 1988, many buyers had no problem shelling out their money for Magadan cards at pretty steep prices, after all, he could hit! The problem was that being a third baseman or a first baseman prospect with the Mets meant there was no place to play. The Mets already had stars Keith Hernandez and Howard Johnson, so there was no room for Magadan to regularly play. His rookie card price softened all during 1987 and into 1988. Now eventually Magadan and Jefferies and others who had no place to regularly play may still make it big, but by the time they do, how long will you have been sitting on their cards? A Mark McGwire card was no more expensive in early 1987 than a Magadan card, and the same is true for a number of other players who had excellent chances of not just making a team, but also becoming a starting player.

In 1988 some Boston Red Sox rookies were in great demand. The Red Sox had young outfielders coming out of their ears. If you threw in a first baseman and a designated hitter, there were five positions up for grabs, but two were almost certain to go to potential HOFers, Darrell Evans and Jim Rice. Simply put, lots of young talent—all at premium prices—but at least a couple of them without starting jobs, and that's bad news for their rookie card prices.

Once you have determined that the prospects you've selected will have a place to play in the majors, some additional investigation is well worthwhile. Whenever possible, go out to a minor league game where one or more of your potential investments are playing. Watch their reactions on the field. Can they do more than just hit? Also, watch other players to see if someone really stands out, as most future major league prospects will do. You also can see a showcase of young talent early in spring training and at the end of the regular season in the majors when clubs often bring up rookies to play a few days or weeks. Maybe you aren't a scout, but few things are worse than buying 1,000 rookie cards to learn that your selected player will never have a regular spot on the roster because he can't field. About the only thing worse than buying 1,000 of those cards is buying 2,000 of them.

Remember, minor league statistics are exactly that, minor league. They are hardly 100 percent accurate in predicting future major league stardom.

Toward the end of each year, the new year's baseball card sets already are being previewed in the major hobby publications. While many of the publications certainly are worthy of subscription dollars, *Sports Collectors Digest* (the only major weekly publication) is worth special attention as the place where you'll get the news of what cards are in the upcoming year's first sets. As the largest card hobby publication, it also is the place where you will be able to first get an idea on the sets' prices, and the most comprehensive opportunity for comparing the prices of various dealers. *Baseball Hobby News, Baseball Cards* magazine, and *Beckett's Baseball Card Monthly* also do an excellent job covering the new issues each year, however, because they are monthly publications it will take a little longer for the information to reach readers.

There are lots of things to look for in rookie cards, and by carefully examining the hobby publications during the winter you can hunt for those things. First, how do the new cards look? Is your rookie prospect pictured on his own card, or does he share space with other rookies who are not quite as desirable? The most important factor here, though, is price. Does the player really fit your budget? Generally, the best approach is to determine just how much money you can afford—and want to tie up—on rookie cards. It's money that may be tied up for years, or could be entirely lost. And, while new sets come out early in the year, the updated sets and others come out late, so a good approach is to save some of your rookie card money for those later purchases.

Once you have a budget you can start buying cards. Co-author Paul Green tends to start with blocks of 100 cards of individual players. The reason is that they are comparatively liquid, at least at the start of the season. For a superb prospect at a great price, you can buy more than 100 of his cards, but Green never buys more than 100 of any rookie priced at more than 25 cents each. If anything, cards priced above 50 cents are the ones where he drops down his purchases to 50 or even 25 cards of the player. At that price level, it will require the player to produce Hall of Fame type statistics on the field before the cards show any real financial appreciation.

Perhaps the rarely broken 100 card maximum rule might seem like it would prevent big profits, but more often than not it's preventing big losses! It also encourages Green to look around at a number of players who are more fun for him. Ultimately, at least in the present market, the liquidity factor also is a concern, and only the hottest players are easy to sell in quantities of 1,000 or more.

Here's another important tip: Don't be a "homer." Sure, you like your local home team(s), and all the reports you hear about their rookie prospects are simply glowing. But (hang on, here's another rule of thumb), those are probably the least accurate reports you can get. If everyone coming up through your team's minor league chain is as good as the claims being made, you can safely assume the club will become the next major dynasty with a starting line-up composed of only future HOFers. It's a nice dream, but it's foolish to invest only on a dream.

Another tip is that patience sometimes is rewarded. Billions and billions of cards will be produced this year—and next. Chances are good that few, if any, will be in short supply. If the player is a great prospect with an immediate starting roster opportunity, then fine, go out and get his cards. But you'll find that sometimes a wait can save you money. That's especially true if you miss a player when his card first comes out; the first year often can be the most deceptive one, whether the player did well or did terribly. Remember the examples of Joe Charboneau and Mike Schmidt. That's where a price limit such as 50 cents per card can really help. If the player has a questionable first year, like Schmidt and Magadan, his card will drop below 50 cents. If you're still a believer in him, it is a lot easier to believe at 35 cents than at 75 cents. Conversely, if a player did well his rookie season then his card's price will rise above 50 cents and you'll protect yourself from purchasing too many of them in case he turns out to be the next Rookie of the Year Charboneau.

A typical example of a rookie card's up and down price swings can illustrate the wisdom of selling cards along the way. A 1987 Topps Mark McGwire rookie card (#366) at the start of the 1987 season could be purchased for about 50 cents or less. As the McGwire home runs mounted so did the price, reaching retail levels as high as five dollars each and wholesale levels of around $2.50. The peak was July of that year, and by late in the season, while it was clear he would set a rookie home run record, it also was clear he would not challenge the Roger Maris record of 61 major league home runs in one season. The McGwire card prices quickly softened to a range of $2.50 to three dollars retail.

Almost one year to the day of his peak price level, when his home runs were not coming as fast in his second season as they did in his first, the retail level was down to about $1.50. By the end of the 1988 season, some dealers were still asking $3.50 for that

1987 card, but with a little shopping around buyers could pick them up for considerably less.

So, selling off parts of a 100 card McGwire hoard over a short period of time would not have made the most possible money for you—assuming you knew *exactly* when to sell *all* of them at the *highest* peak of the market—but the strategy of selling off a little here and a little there would still make you a good profit. It would have enabled you to sell at least some of the cards at or near the peak before prices took a big drop back to reality.

The last step in rookie card investing is the eventual sale of the cards. If everything has gone well, you have 100 of a player's cards that originally cost you only about $10 but now are worth $200. If you are in that delightful position the most important thing to be said is, "Don't get greedy." Interest in even the hottest rookie tends to wane the following year, and if he has a bad season the interest can evaporate faster than Pete Rose can bump an umpire twice. Usually the best strategy is to sell off a percentage of your holdings once you are in a position to make a profit. If the cards originally cost you, say 10 cents each, and now you can sell them for 20 cents, why not take your profits on some of them? If you sell half your holdings at that price you can make a profit and still own the remainder without having any of your money in them. If the prices eventually go even higher, you can sell more and make more profits. However, if something goes wrong and the cards later drop in price, you will have lost nothing because you will already have at least recaptured your original investment. In the modern rookie card market that sometimes is a significant achievement.

The card market of the 1980s was not limited to rookie cards of present day stars (real or imagined). Due to the shortage of adequate supplies of big name rookies like Darryl Strawberry, Wade Boggs, Don Mattingly and others, and the already high price tags for the stars just named, a growing portion of the megalot market has been in the form of non-rookie cards of young stars and "certain" future HOFers such as Rod Carew, Tom Seaver and others who made their card debuts long before there was even a rookie card market.

Aside from the fact that it is not his rookie card, the big negative about buying a 100 card lot of, say 1986 Rod Carew cards at

15 cents each, is the production capacity of modern baseball cards. It is a fact: No regular-issue Donruss, Fleer, or Topps card from the 1980s is ever going to be scarce let alone rare. That fact rules out any dramatic price increases as large numbers of cards should always be available if prices start to move upward. When prices go up, it is amazing how material begins to appear in the marketplace. This is another axiom that has been proven over and over in the rare coin and postage stamps markets. Raise the price and eventually eager sellers appear with the material (unless, of course, the material is genuinely rare with few known examples ever available at any price).

Now that we've discouraged any investors who wanted to retire this year by quickly selling off their just-acquired cards, there are still some things to be said in favor of modern non-rookie cards in large quantities or even in megalots. If you can buy them right, how much downside risk can you possibly have in 100 Rod Carew cards at a dime each? How about a few hundred Steve Carltons at three cents? Obviously, you will have to hold these cards a while to make any money, but if the baseball card collecting hobby continues to grow you're certainly not likely to lose with proven stars. Plus, as we've emphasized elsewhere in the book, these non-rookie cards have much more information about the players, and in some cases, they are the most attractive cards of the players' entire career.

A final noteworthy strategy for modern card investing is the Year End Review. Every year you probably (or should) check your insurance coverage, look over your Wall Street stock holdings and other investments. It simply makes sense to do that with your baseball cards. At the end of each season you easily can obtain the statistics for the year of the major and minor league players. Get the stats and sit down with your cards to make a few educated decisions. Determine which cards you want to continue holding, which could be sold because they are over-priced or have a declining-price future, and which cards you perhaps should put at the top of your want list for future acquisitions.

Let's look at some examples using pitchers because they are always volatile. Sid Fernandez of the Mets is a good, but inconsistent, lefthander. His 1984 Donruss rookie card (#44) has been selling for about five dollars. Now, the 1984 Donruss set is a popular one, but is Fernandez really a card you want to keep in large quantities at $4.50 or five dollars? If he stays with the Mets he may always be overshadowed by guys named Gooden, Darling and a youngster named Cone. If he's traded, how can his value go up if he's suddenly out of New York? Being a New York-based player generally is good for helping to increase a card's value because of the media attention on the teams there. If Fernandez goes to a team where there is less national media attention and, worse when you consider his ERA, if his teammates give him less support with their bats, it could be disastrous for both his won-loss record and his card's value. Now, on top of all that, as this book was being written the Mets had a golden prospect named David West, a lefthander who blitzed the Texas League in 1987 and spent much of 1988 doing the same at Tidewater. Eventually, either West stays in the minors or someone now on the Mets (probably either Fernandez or Bob Ojeda) goes. Even if something goes wrong with West, the Mets have a guy named Blaine Beatty who was repeating in 1988 in the Texas League what West did the year before.

With that sort of analysis (and you should evaluate all of your cards every year), the conclusion would be that Sid Fernandez cards might be very good ones to sell.

With the profits, or whatever you salvaged from your Fernandez cards, there are plenty of ways to spend your money. One good way might be 1988 Cy Young Award winner Frank Viola of the Minnesota Twins. Something like his 1983 Topps rookie card (#586) is not likely to cost much more than Fernandez. Yet, Viola has only been the best lefthander in the American League for several years, and with his 1987 World Series appearance he may start to get the credit he deserves. When he does, a couple of dollars for a Frank Viola rookie card may seem very cheap. He's the kind of player you should put on your buy list.

By reviewing your cards every year, just like setting spending limits when you buy them, you should be able to avoid losses, or at least keep your mistakes to an acceptable minimum. With a lot of study and a little luck you just might discover a couple of good sleepers and be sleeping better at night knowing you made some money.

Down on the Farm

The supply is small, but usually so is demand.

They're the first cards of players, they have limited production, and they have generated enormous collector appeal. They are minor league cards, a rapidly growing part of the hobby. But, do they really have investment potential?

First, consider the possibilities. Currently, a Topps 1963 Pete Rose rookie card in near mint condition will cost you around $500. In light of that, what would a 1962 Pete Rose minor league card from Macon, Georgia, be worth? Surely it would be worth more because it is a year older than the 1963 card, and after all, they would have probably only printed 10 percent of the quantity of the Topps total, right?

That is the sort of (twisted) reasoning that leads some investors to minor league cards. At comparatively modest prices today, some people may wonder if indeed there is a fortune just waiting to be made in the minors. Or, is this an area of cards that is "of collectors, by collectors, and always for collectors" with relatively modest upward potential and just too many risks to justify investment dollars?

The minor league cards of today are not merely some current issue made to feed the hungry collecting tastes of the expanded hobby. The minor league card has a rich and varied tradition dating back to the first baseball cards, the tobacco issues.

Once upon a time, major league baseball teams extended no farther West than the Mississippi River, and not farther South than St. Louis. But organized baseball, even though it was not always major league, was widespread.

Many of these teams had quality players who could have played in the majors. As late as the 1950s, Chuck Connors (television's "The Rifleman") made more money by playing in the Pacific Coast League than he could make in the majors. In earlier days, some great players labored for years in outposts of baseball before being discovered. In many respects, minor league card sets are like the players they depict—a few great ones, and a lot of others.

The first minor league players to be depicted were members of the Brooklyn team in the American Association. That was in the Old Judge tobacco set of 1887. In the Old Judge sets that followed, other leagues and their players were represented. The pattern of featuring minor league players in major card sets continued in the 1900s. The famous T-206 set includes minor league players from the "Southern Leagues" which included the Southern Association, South Atlantic, Texas, and Virginia Leagues. The minor league players depicted in the T-206 set normally are considered to be more scarce than the major league players, and a collection of the 134 minor leaguers would be an interesting and challenging collection.

It didn't stop with the T-206 set. The 1909-1911 Obak sets were made up of players from the Pacific Coast League. The 1910 Old Mill set was one of the most interesting and least known series of the early 1900s. It featured players from eight leagues in the southeastern part of the United States. In total, some 600 cards are known in the set, and there is a good chance that there actually are more because the number of currently known cards from each of the eight leagues varies from 20 to well over 100. Remember that a Casey Stengel minor league card from Maysville in the Blue Grass League exists, and other interesting cards probably are waiting to be discovered and publicized, a fairly common happening with the extensive, yet still mysterious Old Mill set.

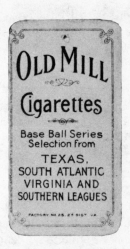

One of the 134 minor league players, Monroe "Dolly" Stark, in the famous T-206 white border card series of 1909-1911.

As the candy makers became active in producing baseball cards their interest included minor leaguers as well. Until 1979, when Topps began its 29th year of continuous baseball card production, the record for card-making was held by the Collins-McCarthy Company of San Francisco. The company, which did undergo a name change or two over the years, produced cards for its candy products, most notably, Zeenuts, a competitor of the famous Cracker Jacks.

From 1911 to 1939, Zeenuts cards chronicled the history of the Pacific Coast League. To this day, many Zeenut cards are unknown. We know they were produced and distributed, but no remaining examples of some cards are known to exist. About 400 different cards were made, including such Hall of Famers (HOFers) as Joe DiMaggio (spelled on the card "DeMaggio") and many others who had their day later playing in the majors.

The minor league card sets did not disappear when Zeenut card production ended in 1939. There are an assortment of issues from a wide range of companies, primarily regional in nature.

These later minor league sets contain many interesting cards, including several Casey Stengel cards, Billy Martin, Ernie Lombardi, and Chuck Connors. As is the case with any minor league set, the big names are the exceptions. Most of these minor leaguers never saw a major league game unless they paid for a ticket to get in the ballpark. That is a problem trying to create broad-based appeal for minor league sets—not that many players became superstars in the majors. But, to the serious collector and the student of baseball, all the "little names" tend to make these sets more interesting and desirable, not less so.

The popularity of Bowman and Topps cards in the 1950s saw minor league sets decline. Actually, it was probably due more to the quick appeal of television as even people in the cities thousands of miles from a major league game could adopt a team from the majors and follow its progress through the season. Expansion into the South (the Milwaukee Braves move to Atlanta and the Rangers and Astros are created) and expansion to the West (the Brooklyn Dodgers move to Los Angeles, the Giants arrive in San Francisco), finally made major league baseball a truly national sport.

Until the mid-1970s, with only a few exceptions, the minor league card sets virtually were forgotten. Then TCMA, a New York card producer, revived the notion of minor league baseball card sets. Starting slowly, but growing with each passing year, TCMA (and later other companies) produced more and more sets until virtually every minor league team had its own card set. In 1988, TCMA made full color sets for each of the 26 Triple-A league teams, a total of 650 different cards. And, that's just one company and one league. ProCards of Collegeville, Pennsylvania, now also produces card sets for all of the Triple-A teams, as well as sets for various single- and double-A teams. In 1988, The Star Company of Cherry Hill, New Jersey, a prolific producer of major league cards for years, entered the minor league market with its first sets of Triple-A players. Many west coast collectors enjoy the cards from a company appropriately named Cal League Cards. Where 20 years ago there had been virtually no minor league sets, by the mid-1980s there were dozens, and that number apparently is getting even higher.

While we're on the subject of Star Company cards this proba-

2   TUCSON TOROS—Pacific Coast League

HEAD COACH—A head coach is a person responsible
for his teams' actions on or off the field.

A coach is the teams' ladder. Your family, teachers and ministers
are all trying to lead you in the right direction. Give them a
chance!

A service to the community from GOLDEN EAGLE DISTRIBUTORS
—Mr. Bill Clements, President and the TUCSON POLICE DEPARTMENT
© 1981 TCMA Ltd. 0306

**1981 OFFICIAL MINOR LEAGUE
PHOTO FACT CARD**
Collect them all!
Write for a free list TCMA Ltd., P.O. Box #2, Amawalk, N.Y. 10501

*The 1981 TCMA minor
league card (#12) of pitcher
Dell Leatherwood of the
Tucson, Arizona Toros, the
triple-A farm team of the
Houston Astros.*

bly is a good time to clarify a potentially puzzling distinction. Beginning collectors sometimes get confused over the term "star." Usually, a "star card" refers to the card of a superstar player, but "Star card" probably refers to a card produced by The Star Company. Of course, you also can have a Star star card, an item produced by The Star Company depicting a big time big leaguer.

There also can be confusion over the term, "key card." It does not refer to the device used for unlocking doors. It means a particularly desirable card that is well known in a specific set. For example, the well-publicized Mickey Mantle #311 is one of the keys of the 1952 Topps set. In higher grades, the #407 Ed Mathews is also a key card in that set.

In a bewildering world of hundreds of recent minor league sets it is difficult to even make generalizations, except that unless you know what you are doing, minor league sets can be disappointing and potentially very costly. To embark on years of collecting fun, learning about and collecting enormously diverse minor league sets is one thing. But to invest without knowledge is another. To spend money on a Nashville Sounds team set featuring Don Mattingly may sound good, until you realize the set actually was privately reprinted and is not anywhere near as "rare" as it was the first time it came off the presses. That is typical of the kinds of pitfalls that can be found among minor league cards of recent vintage.

Despite those pitfalls, people have made real money in minor league cards. The 1983 Tidewater Tides set featuring Darryl Strawberry rose from its issue price of less than $5 to about $50 per set. The 1980 Reading Phillies or the 1982 Columbus Clippers sets sell for as much as several hundred dollars. That's impressive for a set that originally cost just a few dollars.

How good are your chances of making that type of financial return on an investment in minor league cards? The answer to that question involves the cards themselves, and the market that has grown up around them.

Let's start with an attack of honesty about minor league cards. Despite how they look, feel, and even smell, they are not major league baseball cards. At best, we can describe them as inconsistent. Some are rather attractive with good information printed on them. However, most are not attractive. Whether it is the quality of the photographs to the quality of the information on them, often they are less than ideal. (Recent TCMA cards are a nice exception because of their eye appeal and a listing of minor league career statistics of each player on the back of his cards.)

Here's another drawback: As a rule of thumb, when you're seeking a specific minor league player, be he famous or unknown outside the dugout or his immediate family, you must buy the entire minor league set in which his card is contained. In the case of recent sets, this makes an interesting, possible bonus because you just might get a late-blooming star. In the case of old card sets, unless you happen to like lots of pictures of lots of players you've never heard of, it's a small, added burden.

In general, the production runs of minor league sets are very small. Compared to what the Big Three card companies churn out each year (literally billions of cards), it is downright microscopic—5,000 sets here or 10,000 there. That can be good, because if you get a minor league card of someone who turns out to be another Don Mattingly or Darryl Strawberry then the entire set with that player should go up in value. But there's a catch. Sometimes as the price level of the set goes up in value, the production level does, too. The Nashville Sounds example cited earlier is not the only case where reprints of the cards were made. Where a player like Mattingly or Wade Boggs is involved and the price gets high, you can safely assume the temptation to produce more cards exists. In more than one case the temptation prevailed and more cards were produced to meet the demand.

The good news/bad news is that very few minor league sets have been known to be counterfeited, reprinted, or tampered with in any way, mostly because it's not worth the effort. Many minor league sets contain no noteworthy players at all—unless you are a relative of one of the rookie prospects.

The bottom line on the minor league set as an investment is that while you have the characteristics of the rookie card, it is actually more expensive and more speculative. The average current minor league sets cost between three and five dollars, and that amount is rising as demand increases for them. By the end of spring training, for five dollars or a lot less you can buy virtually any just-released card of any current major league rookie. That same five dollars will buy lots of cards of most other players. From an investment standpoint, you're way ahead if you get 10 or 20 cards of a currently promising rookie rather than getting one card of a promising minor league star and 23 other cards picturing young men wearing baseball uniforms, but who probably will not make the majors.

Card prices really are determined by both supply *and* demand. Demand for minor league cards is a bare fraction of the demand for a hot rookie card from a major set. That also means liquidity, how fast you can sell your minor league cards, can and should be a real concern. Many dealers would be unlikely to shell out anything like full value for a minor league card when they might have no idea where or how to sell it. Frankly, some dealers will not even have any idea what it is.

How do you find out about the best of the minor leaguers? Many publications, such as *Baseball America*, frequently have articles about the farm teams and their players. The best of the Triple-A minor league players compete in an annual All-Star game. The 1988 game was held in Buffalo, New York, on July 13, the day after the American and National Leagues All-Star game in Cincinnati.

In the years ahead it will be interesting to see which of the 1988 Triple-A stars moved up (in some cases, again) to the big leagues and stayed there.

1988 Triple-A American League Affiliates All-Stars

Position	Player	Team	Affiliate Team
C	Rey Palacios	Toledo	Detroit
1st B	Luis De Los Santos	Omaha	Kansas City
2nd B	Lance Blankenship	Tacoma	Oakland
3rd B	Tom O'Malley	Oklahoma City	Texas
SS	Eric Yelding	Syracuse	Toronto
OF	Geronimo Berroa	Syracuse	Toronto
OF	Luis Medina	Colorado Springs	Cleveland
P	Mark Huismann	Toledo	Detroit
P	Roy Smith	Portland	Minnesota
P	Mike Kinnunen	Columbus	New York
P	Bob Milacki	Rochester	Baltimore
DH	Tim Pyznarski	Denver	Milwaukee
C	Phil Ouellette	Calgary	Seattle
C	Bob Green	Columbus	New York
IF	Ed Jurak	Tacoma	Oakland
IF	German Rivera	Denver	Milwaukee
OF	Sap Randall	Vancouver	Chicago
OF	Lavell Freeman	Denver	Milwaukee
P	Donn Pall	Vancouver	Chicago
P	Urbano Lugo	Edmonton	California
P	Scott Nielsen	Columbus	New York
P	Steve Curry	Pawtucket	Boston
Manager	Ed Nottle	Pawtucket	Boston
Coach	Bill Plummer	Calgary	Seattle
Coach	Toby Harrah	Oklahoma City	Texas

1988 Triple-A National League Affiliates All-Stars

Position	Player	Team	Affiliate Team
C	Sandy Alomar	Las Vegas	San Diego
1st B	Tracy Woodson	Albuquerque	Los Angeles
2nd B	Joey Corra	Las Vegas	San Diego
3rd B	Marty Brown	Nashville	Cincinnati
SS	Mike Brumley	Las Vegas	San Diego
OF	Mark Carreon	Tidewater	New York
OF	Cameron Drew	Tucson	Houston
OF	Chris Gwynn	Albuquerque	Los Angeles
P	David West	Tidewater	New York
P	Bob Sebra	Indianapolis	Montreal

Position	Player	Team	Affiliate Team
P	Joe Boever	Richmond	Atlanta
P	Mike Bielecki	Iowa	Chicago
DH	Benny Distefano	Buffalo	Pittsburgh
C	Tom Prince	Buffalo	Pittsburgh
C	Bill Bathe	Iowa	Chicago
IF	Gregg Jefferies	Tidewater	New York
IF	Tony Perezchica	Phoenix	San Francisco
OF	Dwight Smith	Iowa	Chicago
OF	Mike Devereaux	Albuquerque	Los Angeles
P	Mike Shelton	Maine	Philadelphia
P	Dave Rajsich	Louisville	St. Louis
P	Greg Harris	Las Vegas	San Diego
P	Hugh Kemp	Nashville	Cincinnati
Manager	Terry Collins	Albuquerque	Los Angeles
Coach	Joe Sparks	Indianapolis	Montreal
Coach	Mike Cubbage	Tidewater	New York

While minor league cards may be a very marginal purchase for the investor, they are great for collectors, whether you choose to go back to their beginnings in the late 1800s or simply specialize in the issues of recent years. Whether you are collecting cards of a certain player, or cards of what may literally be your hometown team, minor league cards offer collectors a lot of possibilities. While they may not be the best buys as investments, you'll probably do fairly well by finding your profits in the hours of fun you'll have and the better knowledge you'll acquire of the game that is played everywhere from Durham to Davenport.

Your potential baseball card purchases are not limited to Topps, Donruss, Fleer, Sportflics, Score, and minor league sets from major card producers. The growth in the popularity of baseball cards and baseball card investment has generated what seems like an endless number ranging from regional issues of a specific team to national issues made by one of the major card companies for commercial businesses, like retail store chains. These cards usually are in the form of boxed sets; the entire set of cards is sold in a box, that's why they're called "boxed sets." Logical, huh?

Now, this situation can become quite bewildering, but like the minor league sets, the roots of today's regional and nationally issued specialty cards stretch far back in baseball card history. From their earliest days, cards have been used to promote specific products, be it tobacco, gum, candy, newspapers, or an assortment of other things. Many times these cards were issued in very limited geographical areas. In other cases, while the company sponsoring the cards may do business across the country, the distribution of their cards might vary. New York area residents would be able to get cards from New York teams, while people in Chicago could obtain players from the Cubs and White Sox.

There is much to be said about the advantages of such card issues for the collector of specific teams. For example, in the mid-1950s, the Johnston Cookie Company of Milwaukee produced three sets of cards honoring the hometown team, then the Braves. The cards were inserted into boxes of cookies sold in the region. You also could purchase sets from the company. (The Hank Aaron cards, originally available free with the cookies or sold for just five cents with five other accompanying cards, now are valued as high as $200. Not a bad way for the cookies to crumble.)

Usually, there is heavy demand from collectors for star players, such as Aaron, who are included in these sets, and many of these sets were scarce even at the time of their original release. That means they might be good, if not spectacular investments. But while you might find a rather quick buyer for the 1954 and 1955 Johnston's Cookies Milwaukee Braves Henry Aaron cards, or the Ed Mathews and Warren Spahn cards of 1953, 1954 and 1955, it might take some salesmanship to unload the Jim Pendleton, Sid Gordon, and Sibby Sisti cookie company cards.

There are similar situations with national issues of the Red Heart dog food and Hires Root Beer cards. While these lack special connection to any one team, they are still popular among collectors of individual players. The 1954 Red Heart Dog Food set of 33 cards includes Mickey Mantle, Duke Snider, Stan Musial, and for those persistent Milwaukee Braves fans, pitcher Warren Spahn. The 1958 Hires Root Beer set also features Aaron and Snider along with Willie Mays.

Although these various regional and national issues lack the much stronger demand associated with Topps and "regular" sets issued by a few of the other big card producers, they are interesting, sometimes very attractive, and worthwhile additions to collections. The same can be said for the modern issues produced for and sold by Toys "R" Us, K-Mart, and many others. Topps, Fleer,

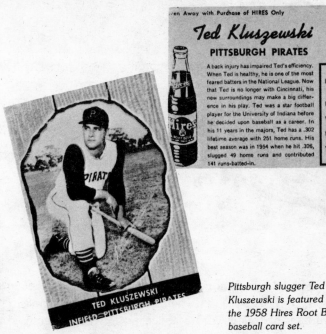

...en Away with Purchase of HIRES Only

Ted Kluszewski

PITTSBURGH PIRATES

A back injury has impaired Ted's efficiency. When Ted is healthy, he is one of the most feared batters in the National League. Now that Ted is no longer with Cincinnati, his new surroundings may make a big difference in his play. Ted was a star football player for the University of Indiana before he decided upon baseball as a career. In his 11 years in the majors, Ted has a .302 lifetime average with 251 home runs. His best season was in 1954 when he hit .326, slugged 49 home runs and contributed 141 runs-batted-in.

INFIELD
BORN:
9/10/24
Argo, Ill.
HEIGHT:
6-2
WEIGHT:
240 lbs.
BATS:
Left
THROWS:
Left

TED KLUSZEWSKI
INFIELD—PITTSBURGH PIRATES

Pittsburgh slugger Ted Kluszewski is featured in the 1958 Hires Root Beer baseball card set.

Donruss and other card companies produce some of these issues especially for promotional or private distribution by retail companies.

The era of the modern boxed set probably started with the 1982 Topps cards issued for the 20th anniversry of the K-mart department store chain. Since then there have been various sets produced by the Big Three for many stores: McCrory, Circle K, Woolworth's, Walgreen's, Kay Bee, Boardwalk, Ben Franklin, Bi-Mart, Revco, Cumberland Farms, 7-Eleven, Rite Aid, and the very popular cards made for the nationwide Toys "R" Us stores. The first major Toys "R" Us baseball cards were issued by Topps in 1987 and featured popular rookies. In 1988 Topps produced another Baseball Rookies set for the toy store chain, and Fleer issued Toys "R" Us Baseball MVPs saluting solid veterans of the game.

Some critics complain that boxed sets always seem to contain the same players. But that is the specific purpose of these card issues, the sets usually concentrate on superstars and hot rookies, exactly the kinds of cards many young collectors want. John Sla-

The Topps Chewing Gum Company produced the 1987 Toys "R" Us Baseball Rookies set featuring Cleveland pitcher Scott Bailes and 32 other young players.

(Copyright Topps Chewing Gum, Inc.)

ter, the "Checklist Clearinghouse" columnist for *Baseball Hobby News,* summed up the situation when he pointed out he doesn't know very many hobbyists whose collecting interest is centered solely on common players!

If you are about to buy one of these sets, and it is not pre-wrapped in plastic, carefully check the box contents to make sure all the cards indeed are there and are in mint condition. "Inspect your sets," urges Bill Pucko, the "Minor Interests" columnist for *Sports Collectors Digest.* "It's easy to get stuck with one that was sorted improperly (at the factory). Mistakes happen, so take the time to look them over."

Pucko also urges collectors to only purchase minor league cards in full sets. "Singles don't command much of a premium, so stay away from them." That's very good advice for a card investor, however, a collector who is trying to assemble "one of everything" of a particular player can be excused for occasionally breaking that rule.

These boxed sets are a wonderful and inexpensive way to get introduced to the hobby and to players currently in demand in the marketplace. Another way to get introduced to the hobby, and get acquainted with your friendly, local neighborhood police officer, began in 1979 when the San Francisco Giants teamed up with local police agencies for a crime prevention program involving baseball cards. It was so successful, police departments around the country have picked up the idea, and that has produced an entirely new collecting field, Police Cards. The front of the card is similar to any other baseball card, there's a picture of a player, his name, the team's name, and perhaps the player's field position. The back of the card contains a crime or fire prevention tip, and perhaps a brief bit of advertising for a company that is supplying the cards as a goodwill gesture.

Initially, the individual cards are only available at the ballparks or, in many cases, directly from local police officers. The idea is to encourage young people to approach a friendly officer and ask for a card. This helps develop a positive relationship between the public and the police, to spread the word on crime prevention. Usually, one or two new cards are made available each week over the course of several weeks or months. After their initial distribution, some card dealers obtain larger quantities either through the sponsoring companies, the ballcubs, the law enforcement agencies, or other sources.

One of the scarcest Police Safety card sets was issued in 1982 in Columbus, Ohio. There are two reasons for its rarity and high price (about $35 for a set of 25 cards). First, compared to comparable sets issued in cities such as Atlanta, Los Angeles, Philadelphia, or San Francisco, Columbus is a much smaller town and one would assume not as many cards were distributed. But the big reason is that a young player named Don Mattingly is pictured on one of the 1982 Columbus Clippers ballclub Police/Fire Safety cards! His card alone sells for about $25.

In 1952 a West Coast bakery with the image-producing name of Mother's Cookies cooked up a baseball card promotion, issuing 64 cards of players in the Pacific Coast League. One free "baseball player trading" card accompanied almost each Mother's Cookies product. The 1952 promotion obviously was successful because it was repeated the following year with a 63 player set. However, another set would not be issued by the company for three decades.

In 1983 Mother's Cookies entered the card promotion business again, starting with a modest set of 20 San Francisco Giants players. Each year since then, the company has produced cards, increasing the number of cards manufactured, the teams represented, and changing the method of distribution. Most of the cards

J.R. RICHARD
(RHP)   50

BIRTHDATE: March 27, 1950
BATTED: Right   **THREW:** Right
ALL STAR PERFORMANCES:

	IP	H	R	ER	BB	SO
1980	2	1	0	0	2	3

1986
ALL TIME
HOUSTON
ALL-STAR
21 of 28

The traditional rounded corners of Mother's Cookies cards are prominent in their 1986 set distributed at the Houston Astrodome or by mail-in redemption coupons.

now are handed out during promotions at major league ball parks in Oakland (the headquarters of Mother's Cookies), San Francisco, Los Angeles, San Diego, Seattle, Houston, and Arlington, Texas. A special four card set featuring Mark McGwire was issued for the National Sports Collectors Convention in San Francisco in 1987, and other special sets have been produced for other promotions.

Don't look for sharp, square corners even on superb mint condition Mother's Cookies cards. All are made with distinctive rounded corners.

Another cookie maker, Drake Bakeries, has been issuing nice looking cards on a regular basis since 1981. They were produced by Topps until 1987 when Drake's printed the cards on panels of cookie boxes distributed in the eastern part of the United States. Drake Bakeries first issued a baseball card set in 1950, but these small, black and white cards are rather scarce.

When you buy a specially produced national or regional set, whether it is the most recent release for a few dollars or one of the older, more expensive sets, you are buying pieces of baseball his-

Toronto's John Mayberry is one of 33 players in the 1981 set issued by Drake Bakeries.

tory for your baseball card collection. If you keep it long enough, the set may increase in value, but it will always be more difficult to sell than a regular issue set from Topps or the other major card producers, even if the specialty set you purchased was made by Topps in the first place. The financial potential for these modern sets generally is very, very limited, and definitely long-term, not short. Their prime value, and it is a big one, is in fulfilling the role of a colorful, enjoyable collectible, not as a portion of a baseball card investment portfolio.

A similar situation exists with the foreign baseball cards sets. Good ideas have no national boundaries, and the good ideas about making baseball cards have crossed international lines. For example, in 1952, cards of players from the three Canadian Class Triple-A teams accompanied packages of a soft drink mix in Canada. Some of the players represented on these cards include pitcher Tommy Lasorda, manager Walt Alston, and pitcher Johnny Podres. Baseball cards were produced in the 1960s in Venezuela.

The tradition continues today. In fact, it has expanded. Several countries now have baseball cards. In 1988, Topps produced a United Kingdom (U.K.) set of cards featuring major players from all of the American and National League teams. While the idea is nice, often times people think they are getting a good deal by get-

Is this a "foreign" (Canadian) card, or a U.S. made card issued in a foreign country? This Argenis Salazar (#154) card from the 1985 O-Pee-Chee set closely resembles the 1985 Topps regular issue set.

(Copyright Topps Chewing Gum, Inc.)

ting a rookie card of a United States baseball player that was issued in another country for less than they would pay for a card printed in the United States of America. Remember these three words: Supply and *demand*. So far, American collectors and investors have shown very little interest in these recent, foreign cards. Until they do, the foreign cards will be a classic case of getting what you pay for. You are paying less for these cards because they simply are not as valuable as the comparable American-made ones. Very probably, they will be much tougher to sell because potential buyers won't be speaking that particular "foreign language."

The Editor of *Baseball Cards* magazine, Kit Kiefer, asks the tongue-in-cheek question, What do you mean by an out of country (foreign) baseball card set? "Do you mean a set produced by a Canadian subsidiary of a U.S. licensee—like O-Pee-Chee for Topps and Leaf for Donruss—for sale in Canada? Do you mean a set authorized by Topps in the United States and produced in Northern Ireland for sale in England?"

Kiefer says most Canadian baseball cards are priced at only about 90 percent of the value of comparable American cards. "They shouldn't be, but they are," he stated.

If you like foreign baseball cards, there is no reason not to include them in your collection. But if you are concerned about profits, stick with the American cards.

Making Up the Roster

Buy good values, not just good prices.

Buying baseball cards is easy. Getting good values when you buy them is not as easy. The frequently repeated consumer warning from the Better Business Bureau applies to cards just as it applies to virtually everything else: More often than not if a deal seems too good to be true, it probably is.

There generally are three ways to buy cards; at auction, through the mail, or in person at a store or baseball card show. All have advantages and disadvantages, and before you buy any cards you should first make some important decisions. Make no mistake about it, once you buy your first baseball card you are almost certain to want more. Most of the time, you probably will want more expensive cards, whether you graduate from three cent cards to those costing 10 or 25 cents each, or from cards with price tags of five dollars to those costing $500, or even $5,000. Just trying to obtain one of everything printed this year would cost thousands of dollars. Enough baseball cards are printed each year to strain most budgets, not to mention all those cards printed in the past century. Once you start going back to earlier issues, your cards can represent a lot of your time and a large sum of your money.

That's why, because of their attraction (in some cases, addiction) you need to make some decisions before you start buying cards. The biggest of those decisions is precisely what cards you intend to buy. To do that you must first consider your budget. While most of us might want to go out and purchase the very first T-206 Honus Wagner we encounter, most of us simply can not afford it. Rather than be frustrated by what you can't afford, why not determine what you realistically can purchase.

Your collection will, in some ways, be a reflection of you. Some people like to have a few, very nice and rather expensive cards, while others prefer stacks and stacks of current rookies. Some might want complete sets, or only Hall of Famers (HOFers). The possibilities are many, but your budget may limit you. It would only be a source of frustration for someone with a $50 a month card-buying budget to attempt to collect a mint condition set of 1952 Topps cards. Realizing that, such an individual might instead seek to assemble a complete set from the 1970s, or cards of future HOFers such as George Brett, or any number of current rookies in lots of 100 cards. There are, of course, many possible options whether the card-buying budget is big or small.

For the collector, determining the cards to be purchased is a relatively easy task. If the goal is a 1956 set, you just slowly piece it together. If you want the cards of Stan Musial or perhaps a complete set of the Chicago Cubs, you simply begin deliberately buying those cards you need to fill the holes in your collection. Investment becomes a secondary consideration, but if you carefully select your cards in terms of their grade and price, chances are the cards will also do well from an investment standpoint.

If you are more concerned about investment, but also understand that baseball cards can provide hours of enjoyment and that large quantities of current rookies with their potential for profit also are coupled with a large degree of financial risk, you are likely to seek some kind of sophisticated balance between collecting and investing. You become the best of both worlds, the collector-investor.

One way to accomplish that goal is through a collection of carefully selected, currently enshrined HOFers. This kind of collection in top grade is about as blue chip as you can get in baseball cards, and would provide those just-mentioned hours of enjoyment as you examine baseball cards from the 1800s to the present day. It also would perhaps do a bit better than a collection of cards sets, as the sets will generally move up or down in price based on what directions are being taken by the values of major stars in those sets. Even though a collection of HOFers is rewarding just for its fun and educational value, it might seem a bit conservative to those attracted by the enormous price jumps seen in the current rookie cards. If you are one of those looking for more adventure, you might be best served by a diversified approach, combining the blue chip security of older cards and a small dose of cards with enormous potential but high financial risk.

Let's construct a sample portfolio for the person seeking this type of balance in their baseball cards. Although $100 is probably not enough to really acquire the ideal cards, the critical consideration here is the percentage of return that the $100 might bring if properly spent.

For $10 (or, 10 percent of whatever is your total investment), you might buy a quantity of current rookie cards of your choice. These might range in price from a few cents to a dollar each. While a $10 investment won't make you a fortune, it limits your potential losses, too. And, if you pick correctly and sell your red hot rookies' cards after they soar in value, you just might be able to buy the rest of your cards in the $100 deal, plus get back your original $100 investment thanks to one or two rookies who have suddenly become the center of attention of the sports media and follow-the-leader card buyers.

For $20 (or, 20 percent of your total investment amount), you could purchase sleepers, cards that apparently are under-valued and under-priced in the marketplace. Maybe it would be the Bill Mazeroski rookie card, perhaps a multi-player card picturing Mantle or Mays, or others mentioned earlier. The big point here is that the cards should have been issued *before* 1980.

For $30 (30 percent of the total, but you probably figured that out already), you could buy HOFers from 1948 to 1970, what many people refer to as the "Golden Age of Baseball." A time period that also is safely before the modern era of enormous volume production of cards. Even with only $30, there are still relatively few HOFers from this era who you could not acquire in mint or

Three relatively inexpensive HOFers: Mordecai "Three Finger" Brown (T-206 series), Harmon Killebrew (1958 Topps #288), and Sandy Koufax (1961 Topps #344).

(Topps cards copyright Topps Chewing Gum, Inc.)

near mint condition, so many apparently are overlooked. You could even include HOFers from regional or other specialty sets if desired. Unless your rookie and sleeper selections are very successful, this portion of your portfolio might very well do better than any of the others in the long run.

For the remaining $40 (yes, 40 percent), you could seek nice, although certainly not mint condition examples of HOFers and other stars from before 1948. Amazingly, even with a limited amount of funds, there are relatively few HOFers you can not acquire for $40 or less per card in very good to excellent condition. Better still, save up for a couple of months and buy one HOFer in extraordinary condition. In addition, you might be able to include a few sleepers from this period, too, in the hope that some day the Veteran's Committee at Cooperstown provides a deserving player with the thrill of a lifetime, and provides you with a pleasant little windfall profit.

Following these rough guidelines collector-investors could combine the best of all elements in baseball cards. In a limited way, they would have the opportunity to pay their money and take their chances in the up and down fortunes of modern rookie cards, and also have a chance to try their luck at slightly speculative older cards. The base of their investments, however, would be in solid, increasingly tough to find cards that generally are more than 20 years old. In addition, at a slow pace the collector-investor also will have a chance to become familiar with cards their fathers and grandfathers might have collected when they were young. Perhaps as interesting, they also will have the opportunity to learn a good deal about baseball and some of the stars who played the game so well, both in the present and, in some cases, the distant past.

No matter what system of buying cards you select, once you have some idea about the cards you want, you then are confronted with the question of how to actually acquire them. Usually when people lose money in baseball cards it happens the moment they buy a card, not when they later try to sell it. The perils at the time of purchase are many, and even if experienced dealers can make mistakes, so can you. The important thing is to minimize the potential mistakes.

One excellent way to purchase cards is at your local baseball card store or at baseball card shows. The enormous advantage of purchasing the card in person is that you get to see the card, make your own careful examination and evaluation of its grade, color, and general desirability. Of course, if you make a mistake when you pick out the card yourself, you really have no one to blame but yourself.

The card show in particular offers added advantages. With many dealers in the same room you have the opportunity to see large numbers of cards. It's not just the diversity of the various inventories that matters, it is the sameness that counts; it gives you a chance to compare the same cards as well as their prices from dealer to dealer. Card show experience is invaluable. You learn how certain cards normally look. Perhaps the margins on certain Mantle cards usually are slightly off-center. That sort of information doesn't always show up in price guides, but if you know it, then you can identify a particularly nice example of that card when you see it. You also can learn a great deal by the cards you do NOT see. At any card show, you'll see boxes and boxes of certain cards, but few if any of some others. That tells you something about their comparative rarity in the marketplace.

Whether you actually buy or sell a single card or not, the time and a few dollars admission price spent going to a large baseball card show are worthwhile. You can learn a heck of a lot about current values on current rookies, and at the same time, you can see for yourself whether there are many Ty Cobb or Babe Ruth cards around. While this may not be scientific study, do it a few times a year and you'll find you know a lot more than you otherwise would about which cards really are common and which are rare in certain grades.

Knowledge about the cards themselves and the marketplace is important in determining what to buy, when to buy it, and at what price. Whether you are walking the aisles at a card show or at one of the local card shops, this knowledge is crucial. If you see a rare card you need, then it may be wise to make the purchase on the spot and not be too concerned about getting it at a lower price—assuming the asking price is not outrageously higher than expected. There are not many cards that you should buy this way, but there are a few, and these are the ones you immediately buy at a big show or a small neighborhood shop. They tend to be from before 1948, as almost any card since that time appears fairly regularly unless it happens to be one that is rarely seen in top condition. Then, too, superb condition, scarce cards can be considered among the items worth immediately buying almost any time you find them at a realistic price.

You should feel little or no pressure to buy 99 percent of the cards you'll see in a shop or at a show. As a rule, it is best to look at every table at a show before making your final selections. Some clever buyers will even wait until the final day of a show before doing some of their buying, feeling that when dealers are nearing closing time of the show they are more likely to lower their prices a little more. Some dealers would rather have the cash flow by making the sale, than pack up the items and take them back home. It doesn't always work that way, and some of the cards you've been waiting for may have been sold by the last day of the show, but then, in many instances some of the best purchases are the ones you don't make—you've saved your money by not buying.

"Heh?," you say. "The best purchases are the ones I did *not* make?" Yes, because once you've taken the time to go to a shop or a card show you often times almost feel it is downright necessary to buy something, anything. Fight that feeling. Fight it hard. Just filling your eyes with the sights of all those cards on display under glass should be enough. If you see the right card at a reasonable price, then by all means buy it. However, if the grade just isn't right for your collection or portfolio, or the price is much too high, then you are probably better off waiting.

An increasingly popular way to buy cards is at an auction. The popularity of this method of sale also means that an increasing number of the most desirable cards and sets now are finding their way into auctions. The first rule about auctions is that the rules vary. A contradiction? Yes and no. There are many different kinds of auctions, and each auctioneer may have his or her own rules of participation for buyers and sellers. There are one-day telephone auctions where potential buyers have just a few hours to phone in their bids, there are combinations of mail bid and phone auctions where the bidders submit their proposals either by mail or telephone or both if they want to change their bids, there are auctions where bids are accepted only by mail, and traditional live auctions where bidders assemble in one room and compete against each other as well as perhaps against bidders who submitted their bids by mail. There are also variations on these systems.

Before you bid in ANY auction, learn the rules. After you have carefully read over all the rules of the auction house, re-read the section on return policies.

Return policies are important. Unless you are at the auction (and if you are, then it is assumed by the auction house that you have taken the opportunity to examine the card), you are bidding on something that is only represented by a photograph and a description of the auction lot in a catalog or advertisement. That description and that photograph are the products of a person who has a vested interest in selling the card at the highest possible price. Naturally, that person may be a bit more optimistic about the card's actual condition and desirability than you are, so you must know in advance what your rights are in the event you want to return an item that is unsatisfactory.

That said, your auction experience should be an enjoyable one. Auctions are an excellent way to fill what are sometimes very black holes in a collection or portfolio. They also are a good opportunity to get items at good prices, although you should be warned in advance there will not be "giveaways." Most auctions have minimum bid levels, a previously announced price where the bidding will start on an item. Without those minimums, auctioneers still usually retain the right to flatly reject any bids that do not appear to be serious offers. No auction house will accept a bid of $100 for a 1952 Topps Mickey Mantle in near mint let alone very good condition. Frankly, there is virtually no reason to waste your time, postage or long distance telephone bills attempting to "steal" an item for only 10 percent of its actual value.

A good rule for auctions or any other baseball card purchases is to set spending limits. Never bid more for any item than you can afford to spend at that time or more than you would expect to pay for the item if you were purchasing it at a local card shop, card show, or through the mail from a dealer. Most veteran auction bidders simply write notations in their auction catalog next to the lot numbers of the cards they want. They'll jot down a maximum price they'll pay for the card and also include a comment or two about the pros and cons of the card if they've personally examined it before the auction started. This note-taking is a major cure for auction fever, the overpowering feeling that you *must* bid on an item no matter how high the price because the card is in an auction.

The final method of obtaining baseball cards is by mail-order. For collectors who live in a town or area that has no baseball card shop or card shows, this is virtually the only way to obtain cards. Collectors of rare coins and postage stamps have bought and sold coins and stamps this way for decades. Now, scores of card dealers are successfully doing business by mail across the country. Buying through the mail has one major disadvantage in that you do not see the cards you are buying until after you have purchased them when they arrive at your mailbox. Most of your mail-order transactions should turn out well for both you and the dealer, however, there can be potential problems. Aside from the few bandits who might be lurking out there with no intention of sending you anything for your money, the biggest problem is over-grading, advertising a card as mint condition, but sending the customer a card that grades near mint or excellent. Over-grading has been a big headache in the coin and stamp business, marketplaces where there are some almost universally accepted grading standards. In the baseball card marketplace, as mentioned before, the grading standards are still evolving and are far from anything close to universal. The grade of a card is crucial to determining its value. The difference between genuine mint and near mint can mean a few cents for a current common card, or literally thousands of dollars for the popular 1952 Topps Mantle.

There are a few simple guidelines you should follow to help make mail-order buying much easier for both you and the mail-order dealer. Again, if it seems too good to be true, it probably is. If one dealer is advertising to sell a mint condition card for $100 while another dealer is willing to pay $300 for the exact same card, something probably is wrong. The first dealer certainly is not just in business for his health, he really does not want to sell the "mint" card for only $100 just so his customers can buy it and promptly sell it to the second dealer for a $200 profit. Quite probably, the $100 card actually is not mint. No dealer will sell desirable cards at lower than wholesale prices through the mail to retail customers. Sure, you can believe that the low-priced card is a great deal, but you do so at your own financial peril. Buy good values, not good

prices. Chasing after the best price often times does not get you
the best deal, or even a good deal.

The mail-order possibilities are endless as you'll learn just by
scanning the advertising pages of publications like *Sports Collectors Digest* each week. Even if you are not actively seeking cards,
reading through the pages and pages of ads gives you a good idea
of the current retail market. Not just what is for sale, but more important, what the dealers are looking to buy, and at what prices.

There also are Want Ads from collectors looking to buy specific items. Just reading a few months' worth of ads will give you a
very strong indication of what cards are easily sold and which ones
seem to be in very limited demand. Whether you're an investor or
collector, knowing what cards you can sell quickly and easily is important because you always can run into financial troubles and
may need to quickly sell all or some of your cards. If they are cards
dealers regularly seek, the process will be easier, quicker and more
likely to produce satisfactory prices for you. (There is an old saying
about some stamps and coins that is very true for some baseball
cards: "The only thing rarer than this specimen is someone who
wants to buy it!")

If you're examining advertisements to buy cards, the question
to ask is how do you make sure you are getting a good deal?
There are ways to protect yourself. In the case of Krause Publications periodicals (*Sports Collectors Digest, Baseball Cards* magazine, *Baseball Cards News*, and others), look for the company's
Krause Customer Service Award logo in the display ad. While it is
not a guarantee, the logo indicates the advertiser has a good track
record in handling customer complaints, if any. A five-year logo
means the dealer has been in business at least that long and has
been consistently operating with minimal problems reported to the
publisher carrying the advertising.

The most valuable asset in mail-order dealings, other than
your bank balance, is the return privilege. It is some protection
against problems, and you should use it. Check over your merchandise as soon as it arrives. Make sure it is the card you ordered,
be certain it was not damaged in transit, and determine if it is the
correct grade. If you have any doubts, show it immediately to
someone you trust for an opinion. If there is a problem, *carefully*
package it up and ship it back, either by insured or registered mail

(depending on the value of the merchandise), and always get a return receipt card from the post office. That way, you'll know when your returned merchandise has been received by the dealer. Be sure to include a polite note to the dealer explaining why you are returning the item(s) and provide your name and address for a refund or exchange. Keep copies of your letters. All of this should be done immediately—there are time limits on return privileges. Some dealers only give a few days, others may grant a few weeks.

Just because you did not like what came in the mail does not mean the seller is intentionally trying to cheat you. Chances are it was only an honest mistake, or that you and the dealer have an honest disagreement over grading, something that is very possible with the subjective nature of grading standards. However, if after politely trying to resolve the problem you still are at odds over settling the matter, send copies of your correspondence along with a brief explanation of your problems to the editor of the publication where you saw the dealer's original advertisement. This usually produces results based on what the publisher feels is fair for both parties. Complaining to the publication carrying the ads usually is a last resort. Disputes often are quickly resolved between buyer and seller with a simple first letter and returning of merchandise.

Even with the potential difficulties, buying through the mail is something done by almost every dealer, collector and investor. It also is extremely competitive. When a new publication arrives in the mail or at the newsstand, many of us drop whatever we are doing and read it cover to cover. Whether you want the best price on the hottest rookie of the moment or a rare Cracker Jack card, if it is something you really want, call the sellers immediately and ask them to hold the card. Usually the dealers will do it, giving you about a week to get your payment into their hands. That's fair— they are doing you a favor. And since a desirable item usually can be sold many times over, you have a responsibility to the sellers and other potential buyers to honor your obligation. Promptly send your payment.

Over time, you'll probably find yourself doing business more and more with a few specific dealers who offer you the service, grading, prices, *and* the selection of cards you like. A good relationship, either in person or by mail, with a few dealers is an advantage for both you and them. You become a regular source of income for them, and over time they might be willing to let you know when they obtain items that might be of interest to you, alerting you about those items before the dealer advertises the cards to the general public. While you may not expect to get any significant price break on such items, just having the opportunity to acquire certain cards that rarely are available could be money in the bank in the future.

Establishing a good relationship with a number of dealers will probably serve you well in your buying and searching for desirable cards. It may also prove to be of some benefit should you decide to sell your holdings. More often than not, if you're buying good cards for investment, the dealer will want to have the opportunity to buy them back when you decide to sell. In fact, for the nicest cards you hold, the dealers may consider it a favor if you ask them first when you want to sell. Other dealers sometimes think it is the obligation of the customer to give the dealer first refusal when it comes time to dispose of a collection or certain rare cards.

Trying to sell cards is something many collectors do not like to even consider, but in reality it is a wise course of action both for the collector and investor as it serves as a good test of both you and your dealers. It's amazing how so many people will invest in cards, coins, stamps or other collectibles for years without ever attempting to test what they have done in the marketplace.

Attempting to sell a card or two a year should be mandatory for any investor. Will the dealer from whom you purchased it buy it back at a fair price—and agree that the card is in the same condition (grade) as when he sold it to you? It's an old story about the item suddenly losing a grade or two, even though it has been safely housed in a protective holder since the minute you purchased it. The dealer may have vowed it was indeed pure mint when you bought it two years ago, but now it is only near mint, or even excellent. If you suddenly find the dealer is not willing to buy back the cards at the same grade at which he sold them, you probably should consider another dealer. How do various other dealers view your cards? Do most of them agree on the condition of the cards? You might discover you have made some costly mistakes. Selling a card or two regularly will give you an early warning sign that you are making such mistakes, or getting less than ideal merchandise from a particular dealer. This early notice will save you a lot of money and heartbreak in the long run.

There is one legitimate reason for your cards to drop a grade lower than their original purchase condition. Poor preservation. Baseball cards are history you can hold in your hand, but they are also rather fragile history. We're talking about a piece of cardboard about as thin as the cardboard liner some dry cleaners place inside laundered, folded shirts. Cards can easily be creased, bent, folded, and frazzled.

Cards are not costly to store properly. Of course, you must prevent them from coming in direct contact with chocolate-covered fingers, the family pets, and polyvinyl chloride (PVC) holders. For years, stamp and coin collectors used transparent, plastic holders made of PVC without realizing what could happen to their precious collectibles. Then reports quickly spread about the damage being done by the PVC in the holders. It can chemically break down, releasing a very tiny amount of gas that will not hurt humans, but can leave a greenish residue on the surface of the coins, the stamps, paper money, and baseball cards. It is not a pretty sight, but it is an expensive one. We personally have seen rare coins made of copper and silver that lost thousands of dollars in value because they were improperly stored for years in a PVC plastic holder. (The PVC breakdown does not affect gold, but then, not much does.)

The cure for PVC holders is prevention. Avoid them. Buy and use transparent holders made of polyethelene, polyproplyene, or Mylar. They are much safer and they are generally inexpensive. The best holders for your more expensive cards are a bit more expensive, plexiglass. If you just spent $300 or $3,000 for a nice card, you certainly can spend another two or three bucks for a solid plexiglass holder to protect your investment. A few extra dollars for a good, permanent holder is a very cheap added cost and one that will be worth the peace of mind for the protection of your card.

Simple card "sleeves," flexible, plastic-like pockets, are fine for most cards. You can buy individual sleeves or sheets that hold up to a dozen cards separately. Many of the sheets are designed to fit into three-ring school binders so you can protect your cards, yet still have easy access to view both front and back sides. No matter how sturdy the holders, you must be very careful about repeatedly taking the cards out and putting them back in. One slip of the hand and you may injure a corner of the card. That could lower its value tremendously.

If you shop smart and store your collection correctly you probably will make out quite well in the world of baseball cards. Not only are your cards likely to increase in value, but you will find yourself spending hours and hours just studying them, reading every word and abbreviation printed on them, and learning more about the cards and our national pastime. While no one would claim that the back of a baseball card is a major literary work, it can be educational, humorous, and in many respects quite reflective of their era in our nation's history.

It's a lot to expect in such a small package, but once you get hooked on baseball cards you'll learn they can be all that and more.

Seasoned Veteran

Going from Terry Kennedy to Al Kaline, but not too quickly.

Once you've begun acquiring baseball cards, you'll likely find that it is perilously close to an addiction. The more you have, the more you want. Do not be too concerned about this overpowering desire. It is a natural symptom and it does not require any medical attention. However, it will require some direction.

Ask almost any long-time collector or investor about their first purchases and they'll frequently roll their eyes, explaining they were almost all mistakes, items they really should never have purchased based on what they know and want today. Again, this is normal and it is one of the reasons why you should probably keep your initial purchases to both small quantities and small dollar amounts. Resist the temptation to assemble in just a few short months the greatest card collection or investment portfolio anyone anywhere has ever seen. It may be a difficult temptation to resist; but at first just channel your enthusiasm into learning about the cards and the game of baseball.

For a while, you will be in the freshman

level of actual baseball card collecting or investing. If you make some mistakes, consider them "tuition," something any experienced collector-investor also has paid along the way. Just seek to pay the smallest amount you can. The best way to do that is to attend as many card shows as possible while keeping your actual purchases down to a small number. Get used to the look and feel of card shows. Learn about the older cards, get a chance to view many of them before you start putting together your Babe Ruth collection. It is very much like baseball itself. You start in the minors with modern cards where the stakes are lower. For example, you might buy a common, current Terry Kennedy card in mint condition before you purchase that 1954 mint Al Kaline rookie card. Then, if you correctly test your grading and purchasing skills with the Kennedy card, you soon will be able to conclude you're ready to move up to buy the Kaline.

Once you've had a little experience seeking cards in person, grading them, attending shows, and following the market, it is probably time to graduate into more advanced purchases and buying strategies. As always, you will learn that information is the key to any form of card collecting or investing.

Let's look at card prices. How much is a particular card really worth? The dealer may have a price tag attached to the card holder, but is the card inside that holder actually worth the amount on the tag or sticker? If you're really serious about investing you better know how much to pay for any given card you are considering for purchase. Plenty of books and magazines provide information on card prices. However, they all have one basic—and big—failing. The prices listed in the publication may be outdated, in fact, downright ancient, by the time you receive that publication. That is not the fault of the editors, they do the best they can to update the card values just before their publications go to press. The "fault" is that the baseball card marketplace can be fairly volatile, and by the time even the fastest working editor and staff compile prices, print them, and mail their publications to you, the values could have significantly changed, up or down. This is especially true with the values of current rookie cards.

Most of the weekly and monthly baseball card publications are very good *general* guides on card values. But they are usually only that, guides. The major publications do not buy or sell cards (their advertisers do that). If the price guide states that a certain card is worth $10, that does not mean you can sell it to the publisher for that amount, or even buy it from the publisher. Nor does it mean that one dealer might refuse to let go of his stock of exactly the same cards for less than $15 each, or another might offer to buy yours for only two dollars each. These are extreme examples, but they drive home the point: Price guides are guides to the values of the baseball cards. They are not Dow Jones stock exchange quotes. They are not firm bid and ask prices.

Veteran California dealer Tony Galovich attends card shows armed with his own "price guide," a lengthy computer printout he compiles sometimes *daily* based on personal observations, discussions with other dealers, auction results, information contained on dealer-to-dealer teletype messages, and so on. Sometimes during a busy card show, he actually will change his buy and sell prices up or down over the course of a few hours.

In the case of current rookies, whether you're buying or selling, even a weekly price guide may not be enough. If you only read monthly, quarterly or annual price guides the chances are sooner or later you'll make a terrible and costly mistake. Here's why. Let's say you want a card, see it advertised at 40 cents each, and you promptly order 100 of them. A week later, you see dealers are selling the same card for only 25 cents. You wonder why. Then you discover it's because your rookie had a fight with the manager and now is riding the dugout bench. That's bad enough, but it happened a few days before you even submitted your order for 100 of his cards at 40 cents each.

How do you avoid that kind of problem? It's simple. You read everything you can about baseball. If you're serious about investing in current rookies and do not read the boxscores from every game played each day, you'll be asking for more trouble than Billy Martin in a saloon. You also should read everything else you can find, learning who is on the disabled lists, who is in a slump, and so on. Every player encounters an off day when nothing goes right, but no rookie card is worth more than a few cents if he's not playing virtually every day. It's your responsibility to know if he's in the game or not, and if he's not regularly in the line-up at the ballpark he probably should not be heavily represented on your portfolio scorecard.

So, you diligently study baseball if you're involved in rookie cards of the past few years. You study the card marketplace just as hard, if not harder, if you're buying older cards for a similar reason. Just as your rookie can go into a slump and cause you financial problems, your older cards can go into a market slump and cause similar problems. You need to know *before* you buy or sell just what a card has been doing lately in the marketplace. The best way to start accumulating that information before you start accumulating stacks of cards is to subscribe to everything. If it's about baseball cards, you should want to read it. You might not accept what is published as being the Gospel Truth, but you should want to read it for yourself before you accept or reject any ideas.

It's amazing how the same people who accuse the news media of being repeatedly biased in favor of one political party or idea will accept every word written in a hobby or general readership magazine, promotional brochures, or advertising copy as absolute fact without ever asking who wrote it and what expertise the writer has to make those claims. If a writer suggests that collectors should buy common 1953 black and white Bowmans, many of the readers will instantly be on the telephones trying to find some without finding out why they should be purchased in the first place.

There have been many examples of authors with various vested interests trying to "hype" certain items in their writings. This has happened with all kinds of collectibles. There is nothing wrong with a dealer writing an article providing information about his marketplace observations or giving readers a chance to pick his brain about his area of expertise. This kind of information is useful for everyone, and without many dealers sharing their discoveries, experiences and knowledge, there would be many empty pages in hobby and collectibles reference works. But sometimes a writer may have hidden motives for strongly suggesting people buy or sell certain items, or support certain ideas and concepts. Sometimes there is more than just a hint of conflict of interest in these writings. That's why it is a good idea to read a wide variety of hobby publications—to obtain a wide variety of marketplace observations.

The same is true with published values of cards. If one price guide states that a Mark McGwire rookie card is valued at four dollars, that's an opinion based on various factors, even though a store around the corner from you might have the same card priced for sale at $2.50 and McGwire might be batting only .240 at the time.

Now before the lynch mob of writers, editors, dealers, and price guide publishers comes looking for the authors of the above statements, let's put it into perspective. Lots of good information is being published, and price guides are very valuable tools, but before readers accept everything as fact, they should have their own experience and information to make an informed judgement on any new ideas or claims that come along. Talk about what you've read with your collecting-investing friends and dealers. Read the "Letters to the Editor" sections of the publications in the weeks following articles that take a stance on buying or selling recommendations. Think.

While the articles and price charts are worthwhile reading, as mentioned before, perhaps the best source of marketplace information can be found in the advertisements of the major hobby publications. That's not only because they tell you what items are available for sale, but also because reading them gives you an excellent idea about the state of the market and the cards you should consider buying or selling. Reading the ads in a baseball card magazine or newspaper is not exactly an art form, but we think most people fail to read between the lines.

First, how many of the advertisements are seeking to *buy* cards? Over time, you can begin to determine if there is a strong market for cards simply on that basis. It may not be totally accurate, yet it certainly makes sense that the market is better when dealers are trying to buy cards rather than merely sell them. Also, what prices are the dealers currently offering?

The second observation you should make from scanning advertisements is what kinds of cards are the dealers seeking to buy? Let's say that in one magazine there are 20 ads placed by dealers looking to buy cards. If five are seeking current rookies, 14 are looking for near mint or better condition pre-1970 cards of stars, and one advertiser is looking for post-1970 stars' cards in mint condition, that should tell you a great deal about what cards are in bigger demand, especially if the same pattern of ads is repeated over several weeks or months. In the face of that kind of evidence, if you then go out and invest in very good condition cards from 1981 then you probably deserve your financial fate. (Maybe you are a contrarian who believes that eventually the trends will change in your direction. That may work now and then, but if there was hardly any demand for an item at any time in the past, there may be hardly any demand for it in the future.)

Want Ads by dealers and the general public, and the lack of want ads, often indicate the kinds of cards that are not exactly a high-demand area of the marketplace at that time. They also, of course, are decent barometers of areas where there is much demand.

The attention you pay to the *buy* ads in the hobby publications actually are helpful signs on when you might start to think about *selling*. If you've held your pre-1970 near mint or better stars' cards for some time, and dealers repeatedly are advertising to buy them at prices that will provide you with a nice profit, perhaps it is time to make those dealers happy and sell off some of your holdings. Watch over a period of a few weeks or a month or two to see if the buy prices are increasing. What do you hear at the local card shows? If there's a scramble to buy certain items, values for those cards probably will go up until the demand is met. Just as with any other investment, you probably will never be able to buy at the bottom of the barrel prices, and you probably will never be able to sell precisely at the height of the market. Don't try unless you are very, very sophisticated and are a "market maker" who is controlling a portion of the action. Remember: Bears can make money, Bulls can make money; Pigs can get slaughtered.

An even more advanced use of the advertisements is to keep track of the *sell* ads to chart rarity information about individual cards. How often do certain cards, in certain grades, appear for sale? Watching the ads in hobby publications can give you a clue. The procedure takes time, but you can turn up valuable information, the sort of information you're not likely to find anywhere, either because no one has been tracking the data, or if they have, they certainly do not want to share it.

Let's assume you are interested in major Hall of Famers, such as Ruth and Cobb. Now, there are many different cards of both that are available. In the T-206 series there are four different Ty Cobb cards while there are four Babe Ruth cards in the famous 1933 Goudey set. In an average 250 plus pages issue of *Sports*

One of the four very
desirable Babe Ruth cards
(#144) in the famous 1933
Goudey Gum Co. set, and
one of the four Ty Cobb
cards (this one with green
background) from the
popular T-206 tobacco card
series of 1909-1911.

Collectors Digest you'll probably see somewhere between five to
ten Ruth and Cobb cards from these two sets being advertised.
The question is, which Ruths and Cobbs will you see? If you keep
track of the number and condition of the cards each week, over a
period of time you will begin to get a reasonable idea as to how the
respective cards stack up against each other in terms of rarity.
From that information you can begin to draw conclusions about
which ones are good values. The same thing can be done with
Mantle cards or virtually any other better cards. (We're not talking
about 1,000 card parcels of current commons here. We're referring
to higher-quality, scarcer cards.)

Don't read the advertisements with an order form and a
checkbook in front of you. We're asking you to do some homework. Charting comparative rarities may seem like a lot of work for
a hobby, but baseball card investing is like any other form of
shrewdly putting your money to work for you. Your efforts probably will meet with success roughly equal to the quality of information on which you base your investments. Just as you would be

ill-advised to act on stock tips you heard from strangers on the street (even Wall Street), you'd also be flirting with disaster by simply making baseball card purchases based on hunches, gossip, or opinions backed by little or no hard evidence.

There are other strategies you may want to employ as you become more involved in baseball cards. A basic strategy, common to most areas of collectibles, is trading up. It's very simple and it is based on the fact that the better the condition of the collectible, the higher the premium and the higher its value. The better the condition of the card, the more desirable it is, and the easier it is to sell at a higher price. Always be on the lookout for opportunities to improve your card holdings, unless of course a particular card has some special sentimental value. That dog-eared Bowman 1951 Ted Williams card could be traded up for a much better replacement, but then your favorite Uncle gave it to you, or you've purchased it from an old friend who acquired it on the same day he saw Williams play in a game between the Red Sox and the Yankees back in 1951.

Those sentimental cards aside, almost any collection will have some weak links based on the condition of some cards. Usually these will be the higher-priced cards, like a Mantle rookie or a Cobb, that you originally purchased in a lower grade because you simply could not afford a better quality specimen at the time.

Since we all have cards like that, trading up should be a common strategy, but it's not used as often as expected. As you attend card shows or visit dealers' stores, keep an eye out for replacements for those cards that you frankly know are not in the condition that you really like, the condition that a dealer buying your collection would like. When you find a better example of a particular card, and it fits your budget, sell or trade your lesser quality card and use the proceeds to help purchase the more desirable example. You'll be able to improve your collection or investment portfolio and not have to spend as much money doing it to obtain the better quality card.

Trading up is a strategy that should be used by both the collector and investor; it's almost mandatory if you're putting together older sets because it almost never fails that older sets will have some below average condition cards. They may even be com-

mons, but the fact remains that they will decrease the overall desirability of the entire set and therefore its total value, even though the
lower quality cards could have been replaced with very little trouble or cost by the owner.

A good rule to remember: Buy the highest quality cards you
can afford. In the long run, superb quality will be in greater demand than average or below average quality whether you have a
common card, a scarce card, or a very rare specimen. In some
cases, that will be near mint or mint condition, in other cases the
best available might be only very good or excellent because there
just are no finer known examples either available or in existence. In
an earlier book, *Collecting Baseball Cards*, the joke was made by
author Donn Pearlman that there are three things to remember
about the value of baseball cards: Condition. Condition. Condition. Yes, it is a joke, but it also is true. Buy the best quality you can
afford. It's no laughing matter.

Experience provides another area where both the collector
and investor may ultimately want to employ the trading up strategy. The experience of knowing how to accurately grade cards
and tell the differences in value between two apparently identical
cards.

As you examine the published definitions for grading standards you'll notice that strict mint condition is described as perfect,
excluding all cards that are slightly off-center or even with faded
colors and mildly washed out printing. The more minor imperfec-
tions seen on the card, the lower its grade and that will have an adverse effect on its value. Yet, you can have two identical cards that
are seemingly graded the same, but one is nicer than the other.
Under any definitions of grading—for cards, coins, or stamps, for
example—there will be some items that are nicer than comparable
specimens, yet all have the same grade. It may be a case where
one card is just slightly better centered, or perhaps the colors are
brighter and more vibrant as opposed to slightly dull or washed-
out, a typical problem with some T-206 cards. The distinctions
may be subtle, but they have a very direct effect on the desirability
of the card and the premium price a more experienced buyer
would expect to pay. You get that experience by personally examining a lot of cards. You will use that experience by trading up for

the really special specimens when the opportunity is there, and in the long run, you'll be happier with the collection or portfolio and much happier with the eventual price you'll get for the cards.

Keep a philosophical approach to card buying. You'll win some, you'll lose some. It happens to all of us, but you need to develop a buying plan and stick with it. Such a plan involves not only the cards you want, but how you plan to get them. Here are a few suggestions to help you get more of your share of the best cards in what can be a most competitive market.

First, determine the dealers who handle the types of cards you want, then get on their mailing lists. If it costs a couple of dollars, so what, it's worth the postage fees requested by the dealers to be among the first to get their price lists or catalogs, and, therefore, have a first shot at the inventories of people who carry exactly the kind of merchandise you want to own. In addition to getting on mailing lists, the moment you receive those price lists and other offerings, read them, just like you'll promptly read the advertisements in the various hobby publications you'll be buying. Baseball cards are not hubcaps, hamburgers, or widgets. Although they may have been mass produced at one time, they are individual and unique in many respects, and if someone gets the one you wanted before you acted, chances are good you're simply out of luck. If it's a current rookie card you want, you'll be able to easily get it, but you may have to pay more than you originally expected. That's bad enough, but in the case of an older card it might be the last time you'll see one—at any price—for months.

If you see an advertisement, or receive a dealer's mailing with an offer for a particular card you want, get on the phone and call the dealer. Not only will the dealer usually hold it for you, the dealer usually is happy to provide a detailed description of the card while you're on the phone. Ask about the corners, the colors, and other aspects. If the printed offer you saw hinted at any flaws, get a further description in your phone call. Remember, if you believe you need time to think it over, you're probably saying "no thanks" to the card. Odds are, unless the card is grossly misrepresented in the printed ad or price list, it won't be around should you decide to call back about it a day or two later.

As noted earlier, once you've established a solid relationship with a dealer, you may become the one receiving the phone calls.

Let's say you are looking for high-quality Play Ball cards or the interesting Goudey 1938 "Heads Up" cards. If you've been buying extensively from one or two dealers, they may write or phone you first when they obtain nice specimens for sale. This works very well for both of you. The dealer makes a quick sale and sometimes can pass along to you the savings of not having to advertise or carry the item in stock for a length of time, and you easily obtain a card you really want.

Understanding the competitive nature of buying cards you may find that it is worth the time and trouble to prepare a short list of your top five or ten priority cards along with the prices you are willing to pay for them in certain grades. A "want list" is handy to keep around when you're reading hobby publications or visiting a show or card store. Armed with your up-to-date listing of the cards you want, their card numbers, and the prices you're willing to pay, you can quickly thumb through the pages of ads in any hobby publication. The quicker you can find what you want in those pages, the quicker you can reach for the telephone giving you a better chance to get the card you want.

More advanced buyers might well find that keeping "census" charts on cards and a list of top buying priorities will not be enough. There is another important part of this mix, the dealer. Charts are worthwhile for him, too. Many dealers are delighted to keep want lists on file for their better customers; that's primarily to keep things organized for communicating with clients in their search for cards.

Some dealers around the country not only get want lists from one of your authors, Paul Green, they get regular updates from him on the cards he still is seeking. To provide that kind of information to your dealers, you must be able to keep track of which cards you told what dealers you want. If you told one dealer you wanted a Lou Gehrig card and you were able to find and buy an example from another source, you should immediately inform that first dealer you no longer are in the market for that card. That's only fair, and it also provides an opportunity to ask the dealer if he has any new and interesting items in stock. In some cases, Green makes weekly calls to selected dealers just to learn what items have been added to their inventories.

Now, this idea of regular contact may seem excessive, and we are not recommending it for run-of-the-mill, $10 or $20 purchases of current commons. But the one-on-one relationship can be financially and educationally profitable. In some collectible fields, the regular contact is closer to being the rule than the exception. Walk around a rare coin or stamp show and you'll see dealer after dealer going to other dealers' tables asking to see their latest acquisitions. In many instances, a new purchase might even carry a slightly higher price tag than it will a few days later, the price could drop a bit if no one immediately purchases it. Even with a slightly higher price, no one seems to mind because they realize that getting the first opportunity to purchase some prized items is worth a few extra dollars. Paying the few extra dollars often will save money, because if the card or coin or stamp is exciting enough, you probably would have to pay even more to the person who beat you to the punch and purchased it first from the original owner.

Of course, there is a difference between regular contact with dealers and becoming a darned nuisance. There is sometimes a fine line between checking with a dealer and being a pain in the neck, or even somewhere lower. You can not expect to regularly call or have a want list serviced if you do not make some purchases. Happily, if you pick your dealers well, they will almost always have something in stock to attract your attention and dollars, even if your first choices are not available. Ultimately, your ability to work with any dealer will depend in part on how you get along, but the best way to start and keep a relationship going strong is by being a good and responsible customer and not wasting the dealer's time. That means if you send a want list, you better really want those cards and have the money to pay for them. If you meet those qualifications, then you are a serious buyer and most dealers will be happy to give a little extra service, and that's to your advantage.

The final key to buying is being up to date on prices. You must be on top of the marketplace. If a dealer quotes you $100 for a card that is near the top of your priority list you'd better know if that is in line for that card or not. Keep your current price guides handy, maybe near the phone, so there will not be any surprises just in case a dealer calls with an intriguing offer that was not one of your original, first choices, but something you might be interested in. If it turns out to be a good deal, you may want to buy it, either to keep or to trade or sell a little later. The basic requirement is that it should be a good deal on an important card, one that truly is in great demand and limited supply.

Don't forget that while price guides can help on prices, it is important to study the market from other perspectives. Go to the auctions, the card shows, the neighborhood shops. See what other people are buying and at what prices, and remember what you've seen. After you've scanned the advertisements for the particular cards you're seeking, go back through the ads at a leisurely pace at a convenient time so you can determine where many dealers think the market is going. After all, they've spent money to buy an ad offering cards at certain prices, therefore, they must assume they can sell those cards at those prices. Compare the advertised prices with the price guide values and see what cards apparently have gone up or down. This may not be scientific, but then the baseball card market is never in precisely the same place it was even the day before. Overnight purchases can be made and things can happen to "adjust" that market from its previous position. You simply want to be able to adjust with it, paying prices that are "right" for the card and the time. It's not easy, but if you follow the market closely you'll discover that more often than not you'll pay the appropriate price and get good value.

Commonly Asked Questions

Go ahead, make our day.

The growth in the popularity of baseball cards has produced a corresponding growth in the numbers and types of new cards, new promotions, and new ideas. All of that means many more decisions now confront the collector-investor today, and there probably are many new questions being asked, too. In no particular order of importance, here are frequently asked questions and frank answers to them.

What should I collect?

In an earlier book, *Collecting Baseball Cards*, an entire chapter was devoted to that commonly asked question. We'll boil it down to the one sentence, all purpose, basic answer: "Whatever you like." There are baseball cards for every budget and virtually every taste. Often times when we are at a baseball card show and a dealer says, "Are you looking for anything in particular?," we'll simply reply, "Whatever strikes my fancy." If you like a card, and if it fits your budget and your collecting-investing objectives, why not buy it. Even if it doesn't fit your investing goals, if you think it's a neat card and you can afford it, why not acquire it for the sheer joy of ownership.

Almost as basic to the question of what to collect is the important relationship between collectors and investors. The collector is the ultimate consumer for cards. If eventually there is no one who wants to own and keep the cards, those lots of 5,000 Mark Grace rookies ultimately will collapse into a heap of dust-covered cardboard. Moreover, the collector and the sophisticated investor are natural friends, both with an appreciation of cards and baseball history. Investors may push the prices higher on the top grade, scarce cards, but that has no adverse affect on collectors as they actually end up laughing all the way to the bank when it's time to sell their collections.

If it looks nice, if you think it is an interesting collectible, if the price is right, go ahead, make your day. Remember, pride of ownership is an important part of collecting.

What about counterfeits? Can't baseball cards easily be copied? How do I know I'm not getting a fake?

That's a good question—glad you asked it. Some cards certainly would seem to be worth the time, trouble and expense of counterfeiting. It would be folly to suggest that no counterfeits have turned up in the marketplace. For example, some 1963 Pete Rose rookie cards were counterfeited. And then, when the fakes were confiscated and stamped with a notice that they were not genuine, they still were sold to the public—and at relatively high prices. As we mentioned in an earlier chapter, some minor league cards have been reprinted, and there are clearly marked reprints of classic sets such as the 1952 Topps and 1933 Goudey that are being sold to an eager public. Wherever there is an expensive card, there is the possibility that some enterprising soul without a heart will try to make a fast buck. Buyers of rare coins, postage stamps, fine art, and gem stones also are aware of the slight possibility of encountering a replica, reproduction, or clever forgery.

The reassuring news is that the vast majority of counterfeit baseball cards have fooled very few, and virtually no one who has really taken the time to study and know their cards has a problem. It is the same with other collectibles. The knowledge you carry around under your Red Sox cap is your best defense. Fortunately, most of the attempts at counterfeiting cards have been poor quality—colors and card stock have been incorrect, not to mention an assortment of other forgery failings.

The reprints generally are not very threatening. Most are plainly marked "reprint" or "reproduction." Some reprints of older cards have appeared as cut-outs and tear-outs in various books. Those cards have perforated edges, like a postage stamp. Naturally, the real T-206 cards and Goudeys do not, so there's little chance of anyone mistaking the reprints for the real thing. Even if someone tried to trim away the perforated edges, experts can tell the difference between a genuinely old card and those produced much more recently. It is hard, if not impossible, to age a card. As one dealer pointed out, decades-old cards found in hoards of un-opened boxes can be distinguished from legitimate mint condition cards of the same players that were carefully preserved after being removed from the pack years ago. Even the best quality cards on the market really do not quite look like they are "fresh from the pack," unless they truly are fresh from it.

Your knowledge, plus your dealer's knowledge and integrity, provide a very solid line of defense against counterfeits.

You mentioned hoards. A lot of very valuable cards have appeared on the market in the late 1980s because they were found in previously unopened boxes in ware-houses and elsewhere. If a lot of previously rare cards sud-denly come on the market, won't prices for those cards drop? What are the financial implications of hoards?

So far, they usually have followed a pattern: For a brief period following news of the discovery, prices can be depressed, but once the hoard's contents are sold off, the publicity it has generated usu-ally results in very solid price increases. If you have a card whose brothers have just appeared from nowhere in a hoard, ride out the brief downward storm as it will only be a case of delayed gains. The card prices probably will catch up later. If you don't have a card that has suddenly appeared in a hoard and you want a speci-men, then by all means buy one if the price is reasonable. If may take a year or so to get moving again, but in all probability the price will pick up again.

An excellent illustration of what can happen is the case of the fabulous Redfield Hoard. It involved coins, not cards, but it's a classic example. LaVere Redfield was a Nevada recluse who left literally hundreds of thousands of silver dollars piled in his home when he died. A Beverly Hills, California, coin dealership eventually purchased the hoard for $7.3 million in early 1976 and it was dispersed into the marketplace with a grand promotion that helped propel prices of most other U.S. silver dollars for years afterward. A similar situation has been happening with the 1950s and early 1960s cards uncovered in hoards in Tennessee, Missouri, and Illinois. Availability of an item already in demand can help create even more demand if the item is carefully promoted.

New Jersey dealer Alan Rosen who purchased a $400,000 hoard of high numbered (issued late in the year) 1952 Topps cards was very concerned about putting so many rare cards on the market. "I honestly thought the end of the hobby was coming when I was sitting there (at home) with 50 to 75 Mantle rookies and 140 Mays cards. I had 5,500 high numbers and I thought the end of the world was there.

"My first ad sold less than $10,000 worth of cards. Then I started giving them away to dealers, cheap. I was charging $2,100 for mint Mantles, $50 for mint high numbers. Then, right after I sold my last card, that's when they started to hit (and prices climbed)."

Rosen said a few years after the 1952 Topps hoard was dispursed, he paid $7,500 for one of the Mantle cards he originally sold for about $2,000.

Frankly, there just are not that many baseball card hoards. Unlike Greeks and Romans who may have buried their silver and gold coins when unfriendly armies advanced in their direction, archeologists are not likely to unearth a clay pot filled with Cap Anson tobacco cards. The older your cards, the smaller the chances that similar specimens will turn up in a hoard. Hoards, such as the boxes of unopened cards from the 1950s, do appear, but those occurrences are rare and in the case of one famous discovery the years of sitting in packs with chewing gum literally destroyed some of the cards. Cardboard can't survive the torture of being below ground or underwater for centuries and still be "good as gold."

A good example of such deterioration is the Paris, Tennessee, card hoard. One hundred thirty previously unopened boxes of 1954 Bowman cards and 50 boxes of 1955 Topps cards were discovered in a warehouse in that small town. "What a shame so many were ruined," says Rosen who swears he ended up throwing out about 100 boxes of cards because they were not even good enough to be used as space fillers in collectors albums.

"We held packs up to the light and you could see bugs crawling right through them, right through holes in the cards. I took abuse for throwing away at least 100 boxes. I got some letters from people telling me that not everyone collects mint condition cards, but those people didn't understand. In most of those cards (from the Tennessee hoard) you couldn't even see the player's face. The fronts of the cards were totally ruined, like a burnished orange from the gum, with holes and a sandpaper finish. They were just horrible. They were destroyed by gum damage and bug infestation," Rosen recalled.

Still, the cards that were good enough to sell were valued at the time at more than $400,000. Imagine what the value could have been had they been properly stored—away from contact with chewing gum and hungry critters.

Hoards from the 1950s are not likely to be found in top condition unless it is a situation like the Moline, Illinois, hoard of 385,000 early Topps and Bowman cards that were carefully preserved by a Midwest collector. Those specimens began entering the marketplace in 1988. After the 1950s you can assume chances for improved survival are better, but the only major threats to current prices appear to be the possibility of future discoveries of hoards of cards from the 1970s to the present.

Are there truly rare cards from, say, 1980?

In a strict sense, no. Current demand exceeds or is roughly equal to the current supply for some cards, but if all the cases of cards from a year like 1980 were suddenly opened and the cards were placed on the market few dealers question that it would have a very real effect on prices.

This brings us back to that old formula, Supply + Demand. Claims of rarity for recent cards by themselves do not by definition mean a dealer is unreliable. Some modern issues allegedly had smaller production levels, like 5,000 cards. The problem is that they are not regular issues, they have a very small market, and in many respects are similar to proof set collecting in coins. Some of the specially made items can be good, but rarely spectacular investments. The trouble is, they were made only to sell to collectors at premium prices. What is their resale or secondary market? While small in production numbers, buyers for these special sets are even small in numbers, and the few who buy them often end up with interesting collectibles that are worth a good deal less than their original price and are very hard to sell at any price. "Limited edition" cards made only for the sake of getting money out of collectors and investors may very well be the modern proof sets of the hobby. Nice to collect, but not appreciating in value much, if at all, and probably losing a few dollars along the way.

Is it an error to buy an error card?

A common joke among stamp and coin collectors goes like this: A collector walks into a hobby shop and asks the dealer, "Do you sell error stamps/coins?" The dealer points to an item in the display case and replies: "Yeah, I made a mistake and paid too much for this one."

Now, those are not the kinds of errors we're talking about here, we've already emphasized ways to avoid those. The types of errors under discussion here are the unintentional mistakes made in producing baseball cards—cards that have been printed in the wrong color or are lacking colors, cards that have been cut off-center, have incorrect information printed on them or are missing information altogether, and so on. Where there are printed materials, there are mistakes now and then. And those mistakes have a long and interesting history. Some postage stamp and coin errors can be valuable, worth thousands of dollars each. Other errors are very, very common and worth virtually nothing above "face" value, the denomination of the stamp or coin.

Some baseball card errors certainly have value. Actually, it is often the corrected card that is worth more than the error because the error card usually was produced in greater quantities than the corrected version. That means a small supply of the "normal"

A mis-cut 1985 Topps rookie card (#536) of Minnesota star Kirby Puckett. The sharp blade that trimmed too close at the bottom and too high at the top also sharply reduced its value.

(Copyright Topps Chewing Gum, Inc.)

cards, and a potentially higher demand if the error has been corrected. The Al Leiter Topps card (#18) of 1988 is a good example, especially since it is Leiter's rookie card and was expected to be actively traded. When the card first appeared the picture was not that of New York Yankees "future star" Leiter, but another left-handed pitcher, Steve George, Leiter's former teammate in a Double-A league. Topps recognized the error, and produced a Leiter card actually picturing Al Leiter. Initially, the cards caused a sensation in the marketplace, but now that adequate quantities of both varieties are meeting demand for them the premium for either the error or corrected card is small. The future values of these cards will depend in large part on the careers of Al Leiter and Steve George.

Most card errors are worth very little premium anyway. The few that are widely recognized and desired can be found in any price guide. Stick to them, then if the error card market expands you'll have some of the best. If it doesn't develop your losses will be small. In the case of newly discovered errors on current cards, the conservative approach is probably the best, and that means waiting a year to see if anyone still cares about the error. In more than one instance, getting in on the "ground floor" price of an error card turned out to be the basement price—with no visible stairway or elevator to the roof.

How accurate are baseball card price guides?

That's a question with as many answers as there are price guides, and perhaps a few extra. As we pointed out earlier in this book, one failing of any price guide is the delay factor. At best the prices are current only as of the time they were assembled by the publisher, at least a couple of weeks before you, the reader, could have received them. As a rule, the more frequently the price guide is published, the more current the prices will be which gives *Sports Collectors Digest* a very solid edge over its competition during times of marketplace volatility. In the off-season, when card prices generally are stable, a monthly guide can be very accurate, too.

Other considerations in using any price guide can be more subtle. Check to be sure that the grades you want are included in the guide, or if there is some formula for determining intermediate grades not listed in the guide. This is especially important for older cards in mint condition. They may not be separately listed, but batched together in near mint category. However, the price guide publisher may suggest a formula for determining values of better condition cards, such as indicating they may be worth 150 or 200 percent more than those same cards in near mint.

The authors believe that *Beckett Baseball Card Monthly* is an excellent magazine. It runs interesting and informative articles, and publisher Dr. James Beckett is a dedicated leader in the collecting field. However, as the demands of the marketplace change, some concepts become obsolete or misleading. The Beckett Monthly price guide has a questionable aspect that could either cost a collector dearly, or permit a person to purchase cards at well below actual market value. The magazine's monthly guide shows the RANGE in which cards are selling, there is a low end of the range and a high end of the range. That's an excellent way to show readers how prices can swing up and down on certain cards, but it also can mislead readers on the actual value of better quality, older cards.

In 1988, when the July Beckett monthly price guide indicated the retail price range for the 1951 Bowman Ted Williams (#165) card was $150 to $300, one of the authors of this book easily sold an example of that card to a dealer (wholesale price) for $375.

Was this mint condition 1951 Bowman Ted Williams card (#165) valued at $300 retail, or actually worth $375 at wholesale?

Why did the card trade for such a significant amount above the much-used Beckett price guide?

The card was mint condition, and the monthly price guide range obviously did not take that high grade into consideration, perhaps because not many mint specimens are trading. Yet, to many Beckett readers, the top price for virtually any 1951 Bowman Ted Williams should be around $300, because that's what was then listed in the monthly guide. The author originally consigned this particular card to a Chicago dealer who was unable to sell it because his customers "only go by Beckett" and balked at paying anything substantially higher than the values listed in the monthly magazine. The author repeatedly told dealers and collectors who would listen that he would be happy to pay $300 each for as many mint condition specimens he could find, knowing he could promptly re-sell them to a knowledgeable dealer at a profit of at least $50 to $75 each. For a smart buyer, who knows that some cards priced "at Beckett" actually are under-priced, some very good values can be found. But, for the collector-investor who blindly sells cards based only on the Beckett prices, it could result in a major financial loss.

Not only can selling at book-based prices be financially harmful, buying simply by the levels shown in a price guide sometimes can result in paying too much or not paying enough to be able to get certain very desirable cards. The mint Williams Bowman card is one example, and so was the early 1988 sale of a T-206 Honus Wagner for a reported $110,000. No price guide came close to suggesting that a Wagner was worth six figures, but for possibly the finest known specimen you simply throw out the book values, whether it's a Wagner or almost any other desirable card.

While no one would advocate that beginners pay above book prices, the experienced collector-investor knows there are many cards that you simply will never obtain unless you are willing to go beyond, occasionally many times above, the current price guide prices.

The Beckett magazine now runs a very informative, two page "condition guide" that quickly teaches readers the crucial and basic facts of life about grading cards. It is *must* reading. There also is a one page explanation of how to use the price guide. That also should be required reading for anyone using the guide. Just as Beckett's has changed with the times to inform readers about the changing marketplace importance of accurate card grading, perhaps it will update the way it lists card values to accurately reflect estimated values by actual grade, not just a potentially misleading broad range.

Be sure the cards you want priced are included in the price guide. There are now so many cards (both old and new) that specialized collectors may someday walk around clutching price guides that are seven inches thick and have a cover price of $29.95 or more. If you're seriously considering cards as an investment (and since you're reading this book, that probably is a safe assumption), you need the most up-to-date information you can get plus an extensive price guide that includes all the older issues.

Yet, don't forget the annual guides. They're important, too. Whether you're an old timer or a novice, it's worth the time and effort to check the major annual price guides each year. How do they compare in terms of values listed? Are one guide's prices consistently higher or lower? Find out what dealers are using and if they depend on different guides for buying and for selling. Before buying cards, check your guides to determine what you can expect to pay for certain cards. Then, go into the market by mail or in person and see what you would actually pay. Do it every few months and you'll quickly find out which guides truly are more accurate and for which kinds of cards.

One thing the guides usually won't tell you is the value of a card that has been autographed. There's a good reason because there is no good rule of thumb here. There are those who collect nothing but autographed cards, while others consider even a genuine player's signature to be a form of graffiti, defacing the card and lowering its value. If you want to collect autographed cards, then go ahead and do it and have fun. If you want to invest, the safe approach is to not have your cards autographed because when it is time to sell there will be fewer potential buyers and it will be harder to sell your cards, especially at the otherwise realistic price you want to get for them.

How much money will I get when I sell my cards?

Unless you happen to have a friend who will pay above the present wholesale rate for your cards, you are faced with several big decisions to make when you attempt to sell your holdings. In addition to answering the question of "How much will I get?," you have to ask, "How *should* I sell my cards?"

The majority of collectors-investors will sell their cards directly to a dealer. Unless you have a fairly important group of cards with a high market value, auctions are not a likely method of sale.

The leading candidates among the dealers who will buy from you are the ones from whom you purchased most of your cards. They should be happy, if not downright delighted, to have the opportunity to buy back some of the cardboard treasures they've sold you over the years. If you determined whether they would buy them back when you first purchased cards from these dealers (as we recommended in an earlier chapter), chances are you'd already know very quickly which person is about to become the next owner of your cards, it should be the dealer(s) you're familiar with and confident in based on your past dealings.

However, if you were not careful in your buying and testing the dealers' buy-back policies over the years, the sale of your cards may be a good deal more difficult and perhaps disappointing. The best way to get a quick test of your cards is to take them to a show and have them examined by several dealers. You may even want to pay a fee for a formal appraisal. From that experience you should be able to get a current price range, and that may surprise you because the differences in prices sometimes can be significant. That's why before selling a collection or portfolio you should at least consider getting more than one offer. It could be extra work for you, but it can mean extra dollars—a lot of them.

Auction sales, either by mail, by telephone, or in person with floor bidders, are an increasingly popular means of selling cards and other sports related items. Before consigning items to anyone for auction, you should thoroughly check out the auction house. Ask for references and then contact those references. Talk to other people in the hobby and ask about the level of prices usually realized (the winning bids) at the firm's auctions, the extent and quality of their advertising, and their specialties (if any). When you talk to officials of the auction company, ask what percentage of the sale price they receive (the seller's commission), the length of time it takes until you will receive payment for your cards, how much—if anything—you will receive as an advance payment before the auction (cash advances), and their policies about minimum bids (so your gem mint 1952 Topps Mantle is not sold for $150). Ask about insurance coverage in case your cards are lost, stolen, or damaged while in the possession of the auction house.

Beyond selecting a firm that is both reputable and interested in handling your material, other very basic, market related questions must be answered: Is it really a good time to be selling your material? Perhaps you must sell and can not wait for market conditions to change in your favor, but even if you can be patient remember there usually is a lag time between the date you actually consign your cards, the date of the auction, and when you are paid. Sometimes there are many months before the cards actually are sold. During that time you are at the mercy of the marketplace, so ideally the market should be very solid (for your kind of cards) before you consign them for sale.

What type of material does well at auction, especially the kind held by the auctioneers I may be doing business with?

While a group of common cards from the 1950s might do very well in some mail bid sales, it might be totally out of place at a more exclusive auction with a primary emphasis on athlete's expensive jerseys and other memorabilia. Other questions about the baseball card market center on the enormous price surges of recent years. If they've gone up so dramatically, will they go up further? The answer to that is another question, "Have you ever heard of gravity?"

Card prices have done remarkably well, and although the future for the baseball card collecting hobby may be bright, it is not unlimited. It is still a market, and all markets have cycles both up and down. Many investors were buying oil wells and Texas properties a decade ago because they believed prices had nowhere to go but up. Today, many of those same people are in bankruptcy court. Stocks, coins, stamps, you name it, they all go up, but they all come down, too. As the charts in this book have shown, baseball cards were weak in the early 1980s and they will be weak again, perhaps due to the national economy as well as their already high prices. Although cards may be essential to our personal enjoyment, if the choice comes to eating or keeping our baseball cards most of us would opt for the food.

Another point worth remembering is that even in a market boom or a market bust, there are some cards that will buck the trend. Rookies like Bo Jackson and Greg Swindell did not go up 300 or 400 percent from 1987 to 1988 like many other cards did. In fact, they dropped by similar percentages, then turned around in 1988. The period of 1987 to 1988 was not an especially good time for cards of the late 1800s or Mattingly rookies, so even in a boom your particular cards could be going bust, or at least not skyrocketing.

OK, but how much money can I actually get for my cards when I sell them? You still didn't answer that question.

That depends, of course, on your cards. Sometimes you may only get 50 percent of average retail; sometimes as much as 80 percent; and as mentioned in the 1951 Bowman Ted Williams example a few pages earlier, perhaps you'll get more than 100 percent of the current price guide value. It all depends on your cards and your ability to negotiate a deal. Cards in both superb condition and in great demand can bring a higher percentage, but you may

have to negotiate and shop around for a buyer, playing one potential dealer against another, kind of like shopping around for a car.
When a dealer knows he has an immediate buyer for your cards,
he may be very willing to pay you a higher than usual price for
them, if you negotiate. The dealer realizes he can make a quick
profit by promptly turning around and selling your cards to one or
more of his retail customers. But if the dealer has no where to immediately go with your cards, if he thinks he will have to keep
them in stock for a while, he may be reluctant to pay a premium,
or even to purchase them.

Is there money to be made in unopened wax packs or unopened cases of cards?

The answer is, "Yes," but you probably won't be the one making the money. Putting aside a case of cards or an unopened wax
pack from 1982 is a good idea, but it's simply a question of
whether you can resist the temptation to open that pack or case.
Most people can't, and once it's been opened, just like toothpaste
in a tube, you can't get them back in. Dealers recognize this and
deep down we all do. Hand someone a wax pack from 1989,
1979, or 1969, it just doesn't matter, they must open that pack and
see what's inside. What's worse is that people know they shouldn't
open them, dealers tell them not to, yet usually within a minute
(often before leaving the dealer's table) the pack is open.

Does that mean I shouldn't buy unopened items?

Certainly not. One of the great joys of life in America is opening a wax pack. Everyone should open a few a year, maybe even a
few hundred. It's legal, it's fun, and you might get lucky. If you
don't, you can always give away the common cards for Halloween.
However, if your purchase of unopened material is going to
cost more than a few dollars, then you better make sure you can
keep yourself from opening it. It's also important that if your purchase is an entire case of cards you understand that you have
some place to keep it, for say, 10 years, as they are best as long
term investments. Storage is important as a case of wax packs may
be more than three feet high. It might make a nice coffee table if

you lay it on its side and have a preference for "late cardboard" as a decorating style. Of course, the drawback is that if you spill soda or other substances on this coffee table, it can't be refinished. Now, if that's for you, by all means buy a case or buy five of 'em.

How can I be sure a wax pack or a case has not been opened and re-sealed before I purchase it?

You can't be entirely sure. If the pack or case obviously has been tampered with, you don't want to buy it. Yet, collectors have opened packs that appeared to have been re-sealed only to find good cards inside. In one instance we know about, someone carefully examined a wax pack with a magnifying glass and proudly pronounced that the pack had been opened. If so, we wish that same proud person would open every pack we buy because that particular 1984 Topps pack he or she rejected contained a Don Mattingly rookie card!

The best general advice regarding unopened material (and all card purchases in general) is to know your dealer. Does the mail-order dealer have a Krause Publications Customer Service Award? Can he supply you with good references? How long has the dealer been in business. (Remember though, that most baseball card dealers only have been around for a few years, anyone doing business prior to 1980 is literally "an old timer.") Most important, does the dealer offer to buy back cards and pass the test when you try to sell some of them?

We've heard about one dealer who is touting cards as excellent investments, but when you want to sell your purchases he sends you a copy of a retail price guide and suggestions for setting up a table at a local card show so you can sell your cards to the public.

If you don't know baseball cards you better know your dealer(s).

What kinds of risks are there in buying cards as an investment?

Most of the risks have been pointed out in earlier chapters. Many of the claims being made about baseball cards as lucrative in-

vestments rest on information that is extremely selective, if not totally exaggerated. Rookie cards can produce stunning financial
gains, but they carry a risk of losing almost all your money, a risk
that is much greater with current rookie cards than with many
other investments. They have an added problem of being rather
difficult to sell for the paper profits you would assume you'd get by
reading price guides. If you are willing to read, study, and read
some more, while throwing in a large dose of common sense and
financial prudence, the risks in the modern rookie card can be
minimized, but many collectors-investors fail to do so.

In the case of older cards, the risks are greatly reduced if
you're willing to study the cards and the market while choosing
your dealers carefully. While there may be questions about the
prices in one area or another, in general, the cards of the 1960s
and earlier are rather modestly priced with excellent long-term potential. However, if you want to get rich quick, the best way is
probably not with old baseball cards, it's with the state lottery.

**Why are there differences in prices for cards of the
same player in different sets from the same year? For example, why is a 1986 Jose Canseco Topps rookie (#20-T)
usually valued higher than his 1986 Fleer card (#U-20)? It's
the same player and the same year, why are there big differences in price?**

Your authors will take turns answering this one. Donn
Pearlman's response first:

There are several sometimes complex and sometimes bewildering reasons for big differences. First, is the "Topps factor" at
work? Many collectors prefer the grandfather of modern cards,
Topps. The other fine brands, such as Donruss, Fleer, Sportflics,
Score, and so on, suffer because of this. That's why some price
guides make a specific note about the "first Topps card" of major
players.

Second, some collectors believe that a player's rookie card
must be a regular issue card, not an item from an updated, traded,
or extended set. Others think the first appearance should be *the*
rookie card. If more people want the updated set's card at the end
of a season then the price for that card will have been run up

months before the rookie's regular set card appears on the market. In the specific case of the 1988 American League MVP, the highest value for a Canseco rookie card belongs to the 1986 regular issue Donruss card (#39), not the Topps traded set or Fleer updated set cards.

A third major factor is our old friend, eye appeal. If more collectors think the Fleer card looks better than the Topps or Donruss, chances are the value of the Fleer card will be higher because of the demand for that item. Remember, too, that if there is strong demand for a particular set, individual cards from that set probably are worth more than comparable cards of the same player produced by another manufacturer.

Now, Paul Green's response:

The first, and most obvious answer, is Supply and Demand. Topps, Donruss, and Fleer do not produce equal numbers of cards each year, nor are they equally easy to obtain. In recent years, less than adequate production levels or malfunctioning distribution systems have resulted in some regular issue cards selling for premiums before they even get to the retail shelves. The wholesalers are getting more money for them right from the start. If that's the case for one rookie, the price will be more expensive simply due to supply and/or original price.

Demand is a factor as well. While Topps must normally be considered traditionally the most desired, that is always subject to changes because of changing taste on the part of buyers or because another company will produce a particularly attractive or (for some other reason) a more desirable set.

Other considerations are equally important. Since the definition of "rookie" card is by no means universal, the price of a specific regular issue card may be hurt by the presence of a prior year card in a traded or updated set as buyers will make different decisions as to which card actually is the rookie. The demand for one card or another thus is hurt.

Remember as well, if one maker produces a player's rookie card one year and the others do not, that first card usually will be worth a very solid premium.

There also are a number of complex variations on this matter. Take the situation with Mark McGwire. He appeared on a 1985 regular Topps card as a member of the 1984 U.S. Olympic team.

Was that his rookie card? The hobby voted yes, pushing its price way up, while probably hurting, to a small degree, his first regular Topps card as a professional player. That 1987 card then sold at lower prices than his 1987 Donruss rookie card.

Additionally, collectors tend to prefer rookie cards where only the player is pictured as opposed to multi-player rookie cards. That does not mean they won't buy the multi-player rookie cards (look at the prices for the 1963 Pete Rose and 1973 Mike Schmidt cards), but if there is a choice between one company's single player card of a particular rookie and another brand offering him only on a multi-player card, demand might well be higher for the card depicting only the one player.

As a rule of thumb, there is probably no good way to predict which rookie card of a given player will be worth the most money. The greatest demand will probably be for his Topps card, but other factors such as smaller supply may well (and increasingly do) make one of the other manufacturer's rookie cards worth more. Over the long term we simply can't project whether the premium you might pay for a given rookie card as opposed to the others will stand the test of time. There just have not been enough cases to study or an adequate passage of time to make any generalizations.

You guys are always referring in this book to cards issued in the 1930s and those real old cards from the turn of the century. I've heard some dealers claim that one day no one will want them because most people today never saw those players in action or don't even know who they are. If that's true, won't older cards be worth less in the future?

If you follow that line of logic, then no one would be investing in mid-late 19th century United States postage stamps and certainly collectors would not buy ancient Roman coins. Have any of us seen Julius Ceasar in person? And, unless you were an heir to the Ming Dynasty, why would you want to invest in a piece of old Chinese pottery?

Just because you grew up with baseball in the 1960s, 1970s, or are just now getting involved in the game, you should not restrict your interest in its earlier history. In fact, the more sophisticated a collector becomes, the more knowledge he or she acquires and the more that person begins to appreciate the classics—items that might be a few decades or even a century old.

The major problem confronting dealers attempting to promote large-quantity sales of older cards (and thus create more interest in them) is the lack of available large quantities to offer their clients. A few phone calls to wholesale sources can quickly round up a thousand or more nice condition 1879 U.S. silver dollars struck at the San Francisco Mint or even locate a hundred lightly-cancelled 1898 Trans-Mississippi four cents denomination stamps. But try to find even a few dozen Charley Root 1933 Goudey cards in excellent or near mint condition, or a significant quantity of any other similar common from that set in decent condition. You can find a few cards here and a few more there, but usually not in the numbers needed for a dealer to successfully mount a promotion of the kind stamp and coin dealers have repeatedly run in their hobbies.

Wait till Next Year

The future

of card

investing

Is it a coincidence that this is chapter number 13?

O nly the future lies ahead.
That sort of logic applies to baseball cards as well as other speculative ventures. If you ask most dealers they will paint a bright day ahead for the hobby of card collecting. They tend to start hedging when you ask them about today's rookie cards, probably due to the fact they know how many cases of 1986, 1987 and 1988 cards they have waiting to be opened in the basement.

No matter how good the marketplace may seem to some people, others will be complaining. Frank Barning, editor of *Baseball Hobby News*, reports the collecting boom has not been painless. "When I entered the hobby in 1975, I heard complaints that things were going to hell. The oldtimers couldn't believe that superstars cost more than commons. In the early 1980s, there were those who bitched that we didn't need Fleer and Donruss and that there were too many cards being issued. Now there are other things to complain about. The more things change, the more they stay the same.

"The hobby isn't decaying, it's just

choked with dealers, many of whom got in too late with too little business experience, knowledge of baseball cards, and capital. They would like things to be the way they were a couple of years ago, but complaining won't turn back the clock," Barning emphasized with his typical no-punches-pulled style.

It's tough to determine where things will go from here. In all honesty, it's difficult even to pinpoint where the hobby is at the moment. Estimates on the number of collectors or even the number of dealers vary. If you gauge it by the demand for new cards, the demand for old cards, or almost any other standard, a compelling case can be made that the card hobby is enormous, and so are the numbers of investors.

In all probablility, the hobby itself is on extremely strong footing. It is safe to assume that baseball cards will never again return to hidden spots in closets or the near-junk status they had a few decades ago. Too many people have been exposed to them, or at least have rediscovered their joys. Cards are fun and in some cases artistic. Many people who initially were attracted by the investment potential of cards fall prey to their allure as collectibles. They decide they'll care less about how much profit they make and more about ways to complete their collections and how they can acquire the cards they need—and want.

For the investor, a few questions about the future of baseball cards cloud the picture. First, cards have experienced phenomenal price increases in recent years. There are concerns, and solid ones, that many cards simply will price themselves beyond the financial reach of many would-be buyers. That tends to lessen the demand for certain cards, and results in softer prices, or much slower increases. Whether it's a rookie card that jumps to $10 (beyond the financial reach of many youngsters), or a 1933 Goudey Babe Ruth at $750 and beyond the means of many adults, the concern is valid.

Another concern is that those involved in the current rookie card market are involved in a potentially dangerous craze, where untapped supplies are so large that, if unleashed, they just could not be absorbed by the market. The supply would far outpace the demand. That concern is above and beyond the day-to-day mystery about whether certain young players will continue to perform well enough on the field to justify the high prices their cards bring at weekend shows. After all, Cooperstown is a relatively quiet little town and the folks there seem content to keep it that way; admission to the Hall of Fame is not granted to those with only one or two promising years of play. It comes only after decades of achievement, and a lot of rookies priced at 25 cents or even a few dollars a card may well become tomorrow's commons.

Baseball cards have an established, but very young market today. No one should doubt or debate that the day will come when the card market peaks and drifts downward, or simply becomes stagnant. The only real questions will be when and at what levels? Some argue with conviction that the growth of merely the last few years is enough to signal a market peak. They point to cards of rookie players who've had one trip around the league that cost more than potential Hall of Famers from the 1950s as a sign of near hysteria. Others point to the price of a Mantle or other cards and suggest they've been driven up in price totally out of proportion to comparable players' cards. Most people involved in other markets do not double or triple their profits every year. And in the baseball card market prices have come so far so fast that it seems continued growth at anything like the pace of the late 1980s simply can not be sustained.

But the argument against the scenario that we are near a market peak or possible downward cycle is also very impressive. Proponents of this line of thinking also recognize that baseball cards have experienced enormous growth in recent years, but they contend that the baseball card market is still in its infancy, that normal cyclical considerations may not yet apply. They point to the fact that major league baseball is viewed in person by tens of millions of people and followed by hundreds of millions on television and radio. Add in attendance at minor league and even college games and the potential collecting audience is enormous. While the number of collectors and investors may not triple each year, the total probably will increase. If it does, with already strained supplies of some cards, price growth in certain areas could be as explosive as we've already seen, and most cards should, at least, have very steady growth. In this scenario, instead of a downward cycle, the market and prices will simply have slower growth. Yet, even slow growth will keep baseball cards as one of the best investments possible, especially if dealer mark-ups are lowered.

So, where does the future lie? Is it all bright, or will we see downward cycles and possible reductions in the number of dealers and collectors?

It depends where you look. The market for individual rookie cards will probably continue, although the rookie card megalot market may not. While specific, individual cards will always be desired by collectors, the lot of 100 or 1,000 Kal Daniels cards is another story. Those lots are sold to speculators. Sold literally as a commodity, like a contract for a railroad freight car filled with wheat. You don't sit for hours looking at 100 identical cards of Randy Meyers. Seen one, you've seen them all. That megalot market is the penny stock market in many respects, a lottery where the losers keep their tickets, the now-almost worthless cards.

The megalot card market fall may well arrive, but it may not be due to the reasons many would suspect or expect. To be sure, if you can buy 1,000 or 10,000 cards of a single player, that card is not very rare. And sure, huge quantities are still waiting to hit the market, but the chances of all the cards hitting the market at the same time and causing a crash are slim.

The threat to the future of the modern rookie card market is more simple, more basic. People buy large lots of a player with one thought in mind: Profit. Most understand the risk that the player may be terrible in a month. They realize his card may become a common, and a not uncommon problem to sell, especially in lots of 500 or 5,000.

What these buyers may not realize is that the player may do well, the card may jump from a dime to a dollar, and they may still be unable to sell them. In some instances, even when the owner finds a willing buyer, many of the cards will be returned because their condition is not up to exacting standards. Yet, the owner never touched them, never fondled them, never even looked at them!

The inability of buyers to eventually sell large lots represents the dagger aimed at the heart of the megalot market. If you can only buy but can't take your profits, it's not a market. As this book was being written, that was close to the real situation. If those who are active in the megalots can establish a two-way market, treating the lots of 100 or 10,000 cards of one player as the same basic commodities they are when being sold to the public, then the future for this form of investment or speculation may be bright. However, if they continue to avoid trading in any secondary (resale) market, the public will quickly leave the marketplace in droves, angry and much poorer for the experience. Such negative word of mouth ultimately could kill the megalot market and decrease the value of cards from the mid to late 1980s because the regular card buyers would be unable and certainly unwilling to absorb the large quantities of cards dumped on the market.

For the rest of the cards, from the Allen & Ginters of the 1880s to the cards of the 1960s and even perhaps 1970s, the future seems bright. Sure, the growth may never be comparable to what we've seen in the past couple of years, but baseball cards now are an established collectible, and despite their big price increases, many are still basically cheap. The most valuable rare coin produced in the United States is valued at between $500,000 and $1 million, far exceeding its precious metal content. It's the same with the world's most valuable rare postage stamps, and they're "only" made of paper. These collector-investor markets have seen prices much, much higher than the highest values established for rare cards. We think there could be more demand for some rare cards than for some rare coins and stamps.

The nearly year-round publicity for organized baseball and the new respectability of collecting baseball cards combine to suggest that, yes, the hobby is still young and still has tremendous potential. New collectors and new money very well could drive prices of excellent quality older cards much, much higher. You would have to conclude that if you wanted to invest in something that also was an enjoyable hobby, baseball cards would have to be just about the best choice available today.

With the exception of policies imposed on advertisers by hobby publishers, local consumer fraud laws, and the U.S. Postal Service's rules, there are no nationwide regulations per se on the buying and selling of baseball cards. But if there are enough abuses in the marketplace, various governmental agencies may get involved and impose mandatory requirements on buyers and sellers.

In the meantime, collectors and investors should become educated and responsible consumers. Here's some advice on how to get started.

The Federal Trade Commission (FTC) and the American Numismatic Association (ANA) have produced a "Consumer Alert" brochure about investing in rare coins. The ANA is a non-profit organization of coin collectors. Based in Colorado, it has about 35,000 members in the U.S. and other countries, and offers many educational programs for beginning and advanced collectors of coins, currency, tokens, and medals.

There are so many similarities between buying coins and buying baseball cards that the excellent guidance provided in that FTC-ANA brochure certainly can (and should) be applied to cards. With a few minor changes in wording to reflect cards, here is their consumer alert.

HOW TO PROTECT YOURSELF

If you intend to buy baseball cards for investment, your best protection is to spend time learning about the cards you are being asked to buy. In the past, most investment gains have gone to collectors who have taken the time to study carefully various aspects of cards including rarity, grading, market availability, and price trends. Investment success over the years is the result of prudently acquiring cards of selected quality, proven rarity, and established collector desirability. Many careful buyers study cards for some time before buying even a single card. Success can also be enhanced by researching dealers, as well as cards.

If you receive any solicitation about investing in cards, keep these points in mind.

Use common sense when evaluating any investment claims and do not rush into buying. It's worth repeating—anything that sounds too good to be true usually is.

Make sure that you know your dealer's reputation and reliability before you send money or authorize a credit card transaction. If you can, find out how long the company has been in business. Don't rely only on what a dealer's representative tells you on the phone. If the dealer claims to be a member of a professional organization, call the organization and make sure that the claim is true. If you cannot confirm the reliability of the dealer, consider investing with another firm.

Do not be taken in by promises that the dealer will buy back your cards or that grading is guaranteed unless you are confident that the dealer has the financial resources to stand behind those promises. Many of the rare coin sellers prosecuted by the Federal Trade Commission during the last several years have not been able to meet guarantees and other obligations to their customers.

It is wise to get a second opinion from another source about the grade and value as soon as you receive your cards. And before you buy, find out what remedies you will have if the second opinion differs. For example, some companies offer a 30-day return period if you are not satisfied with your purchase. Check the information that you are given. Will the full purchase price be refunded or will you be given a credit to be used for the purchase of other cards? If a dealer promises to buy back the cards at the same grade at which they were sold, does that mean at the price you paid or at some discounted price?

Be cautious about grading certificates, especially those furnished by card dealers. Have the grades of any cards you buy checked by an independent source. If you use a grading certificate as a second opinion, be sure you understand what the certificate represents. Grading is not an exact science, and a certificate represents no more than the opinion of the certification service. Find out if the certification service is indeed independent of the dealer, and what grading standards are used. Also, as mentioned earlier, because grading standards vary, cards certified by different services will be worth more or less than other cards of the same grade. Various periodicals list prices for cards. Check the prices for those cards you are considering.

Comparison shop. You need to be concerned not only with the grades, but with the prices as well. Visit several dealers before buying. Check prices in leading card publications to make sure you are not being overcharged. Several publications list representative values for cards of various issues and grades. These values are higher than the prices consumers can expect to receive if they were to immediately sell their cards, and lower than the retail prices consumers may be charged to buy cards. Consult such publications prior to trusting dealers' representatives about the current value of cards. If a dealer's advertised price is much lower than the price listed in these publications, then the dealer may be misrepresenting the quality or grade of the card.

Take possession of any cards you purchase to ensure they exist and to be sure that they are properly stored.

As with any consumer purchase, be wary about giving your credit card number to strangers, especially over the telephone.

HOW TO IDENTIFY FRAUDULENT SELLERS

Fraudulent sellers of cards often look like legitimate dealers. They may produce attractive brochures or advertisements. They may claim to be the largest or finest dealers in the business.

Fraudulent sellers of baseball cards often use many of the same techniques as legitimate dealers to attract buyers. Some advertise in newspapers and magazines. Others use telemarketing, approaching you about card investing through an unsolicited telephone call, or calling you after you have responded by mail to a print advertisement. Because telemarketing has grown so rapidly over the last several years, you should be particularly careful about committing yourself to any purchase from an unsolicited caller. Listed below are some sales techniques commonly used by dishonest dealers.

FALSE GRADING CLAIMS

It is very important that the cards you buy are graded correctly. Because grading includes such factors as "overall appearance" and "eye appeal," it necessarily involves some degree of subjectivity. As a result, the grade assigned to a particular card may vary even among legitimate dealers, especially in the higher, investment quality grades where distinctions in condition are more subtle. Because fine distinctions between grades often mean large differences in the value or price of a card, subjectivity in grading is an inherent risk in card investing. Fraudulent sellers, however, often intentionally inflate the grades of the cards they sell, charging prices many times the card's actual value. For example, you might pay $450 for a 1951 Bowman Ted Williams card which was described to you as having a high grade because of its excellent condition. Later, however, you may find the accurate grade for the card is two or more grades lower, and that card is actually worth only $100 or less. False grading is the most common form of baseball card fraud.

FALSE CERTIFICATION CLAIMS

As the popularity and value of cards increase, more baseball card certification services will appear in the marketplace offering to authenticate and grade cards for a fee. Not all grading services are created equal.

Certification services provided by dishonest card dealers are often part of fraudulent sales schemes and are intended to mislead consumers. In some instances, even certificates from legitimate services can be misleading. For example, some certification services use looser standards than those generally accepted by dealers in the card market. As a result, the cards they certify may be worth less than other cards of the same grade. Before you buy any certified card, make sure you check its current value. In addition, because grading standards have become more stringent over the years, a card graded and certified in prior years may be given a lower grade today. Some fraudulent sellers may use an old certificate to mislead you into believing that a card's grade is accurate. Be sure to check the date of any certificate you are offered and investigate the certification service before you commit to a purchase.

FALSE APPRECIATION CLAIMS

Dishonest dealers often mislead buyers by quoting appreciation rates for rare cards. What cards actually are being used for the index? Are they the same ones being offered to you? Remember, there is no guarantee that any card will appreciate in value. Choose your dealer carefully.

WHERE TO GO FOR HELP

If you have a problem with a card dealer or the dealer has not resolved the problem to your satisfaction, there are a number of places you can go for help. Some dealers will resolve disputes through binding arbitration by an independent third party, usually through one of their professional organizations. Consumer protection agencies, including the Federal Trade Commission, are interested in getting your complaint information to build cases against fraudulent dealers. Although most government offices are not able to resolve individual disputes, they can usually give you sound advice about how to proceed. The following list of organizations and government agencies is a good reference if you run into problems.

The Better Business Bureau is interested in the business practices of companies in your area. Contact the BBB in the city where the card dealer is located.

The State Consumer Protection Agency or Attorney General's office may be interested in your complaint information. Contact the state consumer protection agency or the Attorney General's office in the state where the card dealer is located.

The U.S. Postal Inspector should be contacted if you have a complaint and you ordered, received or paid for your cards through the mail. Postal inspectors are listed under "Postal Service" in the U.S. Government section of your local phone book.

The Federal Trade Commission is interested in receiving your complaint information. Write to Federal Trade Commission, 6th & Pennsylvania, N.W., Washington, D.C., 20580.

Read All About It

Buy the book before the card!

The German poet, author and philosopher Goethe admonished that "knowledge is power." To be a successful collector or investor you must accumulate knowledge *before* you can effectively accumulate cards. There's an old saying in coin collecting, "Buy the book before the coin." In other words, learn about the item first, then when you finally do buy the coin (or baseball card, postage stamp, Monet painting, or slightly used 1952 Studebaker automobile) you'll have a real appreciation for it—and you'll know what you're doing when you actually purchase it.

Throughout this book we've suggested many sports related publications that should be on your regular reading agenda. Here are some recommended hobby magazines, newspapers, and books you also should consider.

Baseball America
P.O. Box 2089
Durham, North Carolina 27702

Not a hobby publication, but a vital tool for any collector-investor who is serious about keeping up with current and prospective players. This is must reading if you are buying minor league and rookie cards. The pages of *Baseball America* are filled with the most comprehensive regular coverage of minor league activities. Readers are also informed about college, rookie leagues, Japan, Mexico, Olympic players, and darn near anything else that is related to baseball. One year subscription (20 issues) is $28.95.

Baseball Card Investment Report
American Card Exchange
125 East Baker
Suite 150
Costa Mesa, California 92626

A monthly newsletter with baseball card market analysis, buying and selling strategies, and bid and ask prices for more than 300 of the most popular investor-quality cards in the marketplace. *Baseball Card Investment Report* is the product of card dealer Tony Galovich and rare coin dealers David Hall and Van Simmons.

A complimentary copy is available for the asking. Subscriptions: Six months (6 issues) $17; one year (12 issues) $29; and two years (24 issues) $49.

Baseball Card News
700 East State Street
Iola, Wisconsin 54990

An excellent newspaper for the beginner, it covers all types of sports collectibles with emphasis on baseball cards, autographs, photos, yearbooks, ticket stubs, players' uniforms, and other sports souvenirs of baseball, football, basketball, hockey, boxing, basketball and some non-sports areas, too. Originally published monthly, *Baseball Card News* now comes out every two weeks.

A sample copy is available from the publisher for only $1.00. Subscriptions: One year (26 issues) $21.50.

Baseball Cards Magazine
700 East State Street
Iola, Wisconsin 54990

Underscoring the tremendous increase in card collecting, this publication switched in 1987 from producing four issues a year to become a monthly magazine. Each issue has a price guide for major cards produced since 1948, about a half dozen special articles about cards and players, and interesting features such as the "Collector Q&A" department. Frequent use of full-color photographs of various cards and players and Editor Kit Kiefer's witty comments make the magazine even more lively.

Single issue newsstand cover price is $2.50 per copy. Subscriptions: One year (12 issues) $15.95; two years (24 issues) $29.95; and three years (36 issues) $42.00.

Baseball Hobby News
4540 Kearny Villa Road
Suite 215
San Diego, California 92123-1573

Started in 1979, this thick, monthly tabloid covers a wide range of baseball collectibles with a fine mix of current news about cards, research, educational features, regular columnists writing on many hobby topics, and a price guide for the rookie cards of former and current major league players. Founders Frank and Vivian Barning offer no-punches-pulled, knowledgeable opinions about the hobby and the baseball card marketplace. Readers are always encouraged to voice their opinions, too.

Readers of this book may request a sample copy for only $1.00. Subscriptions: six months (6 issues) $9.95; one year (12 issues) $18.00; and two years (24 issues) $34.00,

Beckett Baseball Card Monthly
3410 MidCourt
Suite 110
Carrollton, Texas 75006

This is an extremely popular publication produced by the prominent collector and baseball card researcher, Dr. James Beckett. The magazine is issued every month. Its fine articles and regular columns give a sense of historical perspective to the game of baseball and the cards that reflect that history. A regular feature, the "Weather Report," has been expanded to provide even more information about the "temperature" ranking of which players, teams, and baseball card sets are hot and which are not, according to readers across the country. (Sometimes a player, such as Eric Davis, gets ranked on both lists because some readers think he's hot, others claim he's cold.) The centerpiece of the magazine is an updated card price guide compiled by Dr. Beckett and his staff. While the format of the price guide may be somewhat misleading, the magazine's excellent condition (grading) guide section is worth the cover price.

Cover price is $2.50. Subscriptions: One year (12 issues) $19.95; two years (24 issues) $35.95; three years (36 issues) $47.95; and four years (48 issues) $59.95.

Sports Collectors Digest
700 East State Street
Iola, Wisconsin 54990

Yet, another outstanding publication from the hobby writers and editors at Krause Publications in the small northern Wisconsin community of Iola. With an updated price guide in each almost-tabloid-sized issue every week, those writers and Publisher Bob Lemke keep the keyboards and the calculators busy. Each thick issue runs about 180 pages and is filled with advertisements and late-breaking news about new card issues, readers' questions (and the editors' answers), feature articles, and usually lots of black and white photos of cards and ballplayers. *Sports Collectors Digest* is the hobby's largest and oldest publication.

Single copy price is $2.95. Subscriptions: Six months (26 issues) $15.50; one year (52 issues) $29.95; two years (104 issues) $55.50; and three years (156 issues) $79.95.

The Old Judge
c/o Lew Lipset
P.O. Box 137
Centereach, New York 11720

An informative newsletter that serves as an update for the very important *Encyclopedia of Baseball Cards*. The Old Judge, named after the "first" tobacco cards, provides comments on current hobby trends, book reviews, articles about cards and baseball memorabilia, and price guide information on pre-World War II baseball cards.

Sample copies are available for $2.00 each. Subscriptions: One year (six issues) $8.00; two years (12 issues) $15.00 .

Tuff-Stuff
Box 1637
Glen Allen, Virginia 23060

A relative newcomer to the hobby field, this monthly magazine has quickly grown in pages and popularity. Among its regular features are "The Rookie Roster" (a price guide for current rookies' cards), a value guide for minor league card sets issued since 1960, and stories about cards and ballplayers.

Subscriptions: Six month (6 issues) $9.95; one year (12 issues) $17.95; and two years (24 issues) $31.95.

Casual *and* serious collectors should also add a few important research books to their personal libraries.

The *Sports Collectors Digest Baseball Card Price Guide* is an annual, illustrated guide (first published in 1987) that lists 200,000 prices for more than 70,000 of the most popular cards. It is sold at hobby stores and most major book store chains, and available from *Sports Collectors Digest* (see address above). Suggested retail price is $12.95

New for 1989 is the *Standard Catalog of Baseball Cards* also from Krause Publications (the folks who produce *Sports Collectors Digest* and many other hobby publications). In addition to an extensive listing of cards similar to the company's new, annual price guide, this encyclopedia also includes many minor league sets and "obscure regional issues going back to the 1880s," according to publisher Bob Lemke. This is the most comprehensive book ever produced on baseball cards and their values. Suggested retail price is $24.95.

A fabulous coffeetable book, *Topps Baseball Cards: A 35 Year History 1951-1985* puts full-color illustrations of all 22,000 Topps cards from that time period at your fingertips in 1,300 pages. The book usually sells for about $75, but some bookstores and card dealers have offered copies for as little as $59 each. It is a delightful way to finally own an entire Topps 1952 set of cards!

Another big volume is *The Complete Book of Collectible Baseball Cards* by the editors of Consumer Guide. While the book is certainly not "complete," it is extensive and you'll discover a wonderful overview of cards in its 400 or so pages. Even though the book was revised in 1987, the price guide information is outdated, but the factual narrative is excellent. Many illustrations, including 40 pages in color. Published by Beekman House, New York, and distributed by Crown Publishers, New York.

A three-volume set, *Encyclopedia of Baseball Cards* traces the history of cards from the 19th century (volume one $11.95) to the early gum and candy cards (volume two $11.95) and through the 20th century tobacco cards (volume three $12.95). They are sold through Lew Lipset (see *The Old Judge* address above and add $3.00 per order for U.P.S. delivery charges). The books are also sold by Beckett Publications.

Dr. Beckett also offers collectors many other very useful books that are featured in ads in each issue of *Beckett Baseball Card Monthly*. Among the handiest is *The Sport Americana Alphabetical Baseball Card Checklist #3*. For only $9.95 you have a vital, 292 page reference book matching major and minor league players with their baseball cards by card issuer, year of issue, and card number. There are more than 85,000 cards in this reference work. If you are serious about collecting or investing in cards, you need this book. Another important reference volume is the 10th edition of *The Sport Americana Baseball Card Price Guide* with 580 pages of values for thousands of different cards. It is priced at $12.95. These books and other hobby price guides are available from Beckett Publications, 3410 MidCourt, Suite 110, Carrollton, Texas 75006. Add $1 per book for postage.

A Few Final Thoughts

On the final

few pages

We hope this book gives you a big hand.

How often can you make money doing something you really like? For most people, the answer is not very often. Jobs usually are work, not play. Most people find nothing particularly special about their investments except the bottom line.

Baseball cards are different. They are fun and play. Yet, they can be good investments.

In that stack of old cards you can literally see the history of America's national pastime, and, in a way, the history of the land and its people. Look at that faded card of "Smokey" Joe Wood, a brilliant pitcher who brought a championship to the Red Sox by winning three of Boston's four World Series victories against the New York Giants in 1912, the year they opened Fenway Park. His great pitching career was cut short, but he returned to the game as a successful outfielder. Remember as you look into his eyes, that this man (with the exception of Jim Thorpe) might have been the best athlete of his day. And remember, too, that Joe Wood traveled in a covered wagon, but lived long enough to see men land on the moon.

The smile of Lou Gehrig (1933 Goudey #92) and the royalty of "Joltin' " Joe DiMaggio (1941 Play Ball #71).

Look at a T-206 of Ty Cobb and see the man. A man possessed on the field and haunted by the demons of a family tragedy where his mother killed his father. Tyrus Raymond Cobb has a special place in the game's history even though he had few allies and even fewer friends.

Look at a 1933 Goudey card of Babe Ruth. The Babe who loomed larger than life on the field and off, then and now. The cards reflect the classic image of the man. They don't even need to be labeled, for you know at a glance, these are the cards of Babe Ruth.

Look, too, at a 1933 Goudey of Lou Gehrig, the iron horse, the power and the strength are there, but so is the smile of a man who virtually was without enemies.

It goes on like that with almost any baseball card. Look at the 1941 Play Ball card of Joe DiMaggio; the figure is lean, the background an appropriate purple, the color of royalty. Indeed, for America of World War II and after, Joe DiMaggio came about as close as we get to royalty. Even today, Joe DiMaggio remains someone and something special: The man who got a hit in 56 straight games, the man who married Marilyn Monroe, the man who could just about do anything at a time the country figured it, too, could accomplish whatever was needed.

Look at some of the cards of the 1950s. The 1953 Topps of Satchel Paige tells a story. The man on the card is not a young kid, and the Lord only knows how old he really was. We just know that for decades that man was kept out of the game because of the color of that aging skin. Like so many others, Paige seemed to harbor no ill feelings. Perhaps he knew that while he was kept out of the major leagues, Satchel Paige was not the only one to suffer. The game suffered. The fans suffered. And even today, the unfortunate legacy is felt as baseball card collectors try to add to their collection one of the few cards (the 1953 Topps #220 being the most common) of perhaps the greatest pitcher of all time.

Look through those cards of the 1950s. The Boys of Summer stare out at you in set after set, year after year, waiting until next year while the Yankees took the championship. Today, those Mickey Mantles—not the Jackie Robinsons, Roy Campanellas or Duke Sniders—take the prices at card shows.

Look at those 1955 Bowman television cards. Some of them have umpires on them. No such cards would be produced in the 1970s. You look at gray borders on 1970 cards, you look to find the almost impossible-to-locate unchipped black borders of 1971. And, the most unusual of all, those 1972 Topps designs. You can't really describe a 1972 card, you have to experience it. If one of them had been produced in the 1950s, it might have been put on trial. The same might be said of the colors used for backgrounds in 1975. You could call them bright, and you just might wonder if that was the period when a guy named Charlie Finley (with a mule as a mascot) was tinkering around with the idea of orange-colored baseballs and, you guessed it, colorful uniforms.

It's not just a case of the greats. As the collector of full sets knows so well, you'll have lots of fun with the not-so-greats. Maybe it's a minor league card from the T-206 set. Perhaps a Washington Senators team card. The possibilities are nearly endless. From the caps of Charles Comiskey and the others pictured on the Allen & Ginter or "Old Judge" cards, to the brief time during the 1970s when the Chicago White Sox brought back the old time style, the

Frivolous and fabulous moments in baseball history captured on cards.

(Topps cards copyright Topps Chewing Gum, Inc.)

baseball card reflects a passing parade of players, baseball fashions, baseball equipment, history, and hope.

You can find some of baseball's lighter side on cards, too. The 1976 Topps card (#564) features the 1975 bubble gum blowing champion, Milwaukee's Kurt Bevacqua. Cubs' funnyman Jay Johnstone wears a hat decorated with Budweiser brand beer labels on his 1984 Fleer card (#495), while on his 1986 Fleer card (#396), Minnesota's Mickey Hatcher demonstrates how easy it is to work the outfield with a slightly oversized glove (see page 214).

And, oh, those classic moments captured on cards—like the 1954 World Series Willie Mays' catch of Vic Wertz's drive, and Stan Musial's 3,000th career hit. There are all those recent tributes to Pete Rose as he surpassed Ty Cobb's all-time hit record. One of the best is the 1986 Donruss (#644) showing Rose getting both the record-tying hit number 4,191 and the record-setting 4,192.

Whatever your particular interests in baseball history, you can almost certainly find them represented somewhere on baseball cards, often in unusual ways.

Whether your area of concentration and specialization is the completion of certain sets, your favorite team, Hall of Famers, or even the modern cards of promising rookies, if you're going to do it right you had better plan on spending a lot of time reading and researching. This study is not work in the strict sense, in fact, for collectors it should be something closer to a treasure hunt. It is hardly work if you love baseball.

Another positive point, and one that may be overlooked, is that baseball card investing is democratic. The card market has room for the buyer with $10 or $100,000 a month, and chances are excellent that the low-budget investor will do as well if not better than the buyer with a bank balance close to that of George Steinbrenner. Of course, the downside risk of what you can lose is what you want to make it. You can risk a few dollars or you can risk a bundle, but either way it is your own choice.

Ease of entry into the market is a major factor that attracts many to baseball card collecting. Yet, there are other factors. Unlike some investments, baseball card purchases are as good as you make them. Unless you're a scout for a major league team, the information available to you on a young player is identical to the information available to everyone else. In baseball card investing there need be no expensive investment advisors when it comes to projecting the future of currently active players. A similar situation exists in the case of players from the past.

While there are dealers with an excellent feel for the market and who have keen grading skills, you can do plenty to compensate for a lack of money or hands-on experience. One thing you can do that will likely help both your investment and your baseball knowledge is to seek undervalued stars among the players prior to 1970. There are plenty of them, from inexpensive HOFers to others with anywhere from a good to an outside chance of getting into Cooperstown. If you want to maximize your profit potential then concentrate your studies on players from around 1935 to 1960, that's the period most current members of the Hall of Fame Veteran's Committee would remember best. If you want to make some real long shots, look at even earlier periods where you can find plenty of lifetime .300 hitters who are not in the Hall of Fame. (Remember, if they're from an era before the early 1920s, you shouldn't count their home run totals because it was the era of the dead ball.)

No topic is more interesting and potentially rewarding than that of the actual rarity of specific cards within certain sets. It is a field wide open for debate with relatively little known about it. The T-206 Ty Cobb card with a green background is just one example from literally hundreds of potential areas for research. Sure, more has been written about the T-206 set than perhaps any other, yet dealers and specialists still spend hours discussing and debating how rare or scarce certain cards in that set are compared to others. The same could be said for the rarity of Goudeys, caramel cards, and almost any issues before 1948. The person willing to study a specific set probably can make some excellent purchases on the basis of knowledge—a great equalizer, when your funds are limited.

It can be a fascinating search for anyone willing to spend the time, and can result in a card collection of stars who deserve to be in Cooperstown. If carefully selected, they'd make an interesting collection, a fairly solid investment, and the owner of these cards would have accumulated very solid baseball knowledge.

Just as it's a treasure hunt to spot tomorrow's HOFers, it's also a treasure hunt to spot genuinely rare cards. In the case of many sets, there are checklists, but still no real idea about how truly elusive many of the cards really are today. Even if we assume they were printed in equal numbers (which was not always the case) we have no real idea how many of a specific card might have survived over the years. Dealers develop a certain sense about the cards they regularly see and ones they don't see as often, but they don't have scientific, precise information about card rarity. While your own studies may not be totally scientific, in many ways you can monitor existing supplies of cards and that will enable you to pick off legitimately tough-to-find cards, often at bargain prices.

There's your treasure hunt. You seek the potentially excellent buys that we all know are out there. Your map for this hunt is the knowledge you manage to accumulate. It's the knowledge of baseball as it is today, as it's been in the past, and it's the key to unlocking profits that will be in baseball cards tomorrow.

For centuries, people have searched for a Fountain of Youth, a mythical place where you become young again no matter what your age or physical condition. Today, that mythical place is as close as a wax pack. Open a pack and you can feel the power of the baseball card cure. For a brief moment, that simple activity makes anyone young again. The best part is that the magic powers are not limited to today's wax packs. Take out your favorite cards from whatever era and take a long look. Through those pieces of cardboard you are transported to times long past. Stare at a 1956 Herb Score (Topps #140) and you can almost feel the music and remember that in 1956 Score was just about the best pitcher anyone had ever seen. Look at an early Willie Mays and you can still see him in your mind, playing the game like no one else. Look at any 1969 Mets player and recall the "Miracle Mets" who won the World Series. Hold a Kent Hrbek, Kirby Puckett, or Frank Viola card and remember the 1987 World Series.

Whatever your age, your youth is waiting to come alive with baseball cards. Ruth still connects, DiMaggio still hits, Stan is still "The Man," Koufax still mows them down, and Ernie Banks still wants to play two today. In the presence of a childhood idol you are young, if only for a moment. A whole generation is now learning that it can go back, way back, and remember and rejoice in the summers that were.

The combination of profit potential, pride in a collection, personal recollections being brought to life, and the history of the game all make baseball cards a winner—no matter what your financial league.

We hope this book gives you "a big hand."

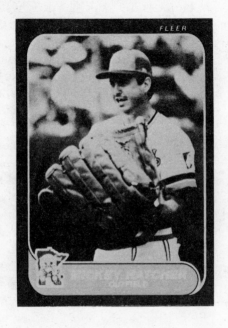

ABOUT THE AUTHORS

PAUL M. GREEN received a Lifetime Pass to the Baseball Hall of Fame for his outstanding sports writing. He has conducted nearly 100 interviews of veteran players for profile stories in *Sports Collectors Digest* and his byline also is frequently seen in *Baseball Cards* magazine as well as other major hobby publications. He closely covers the card marketplace and assisted in the writing of the Krause S.C.D. *Baseball Card Price Guide*. His coin collecting and investing articles have received numerous awards from the Numismatic Literary Guild.

Green is the author of two baseball books, *Forgotten Fields* and *The Battles of Bunker Hill*. He is a member of the Joe Jackson Society and the Major League Players Alumni Association.

DONN PEARLMAN is an award-winning broadcaster and hobby writer. He has been cited by the Associated Press as "Reporter of the Year" and his work also has been honored by United Press International, the Radio-TV News Directors Association, and the Chicago Headline Club.

In 1986, Pearlman was selected as one of the 20 Midwest semi-finalists for NASA's Journalist-in-Space program.

Pearlman is the author of two earlier books, *Breaking into Broadcasting* and *Collecting Baseball Cards*. He is a contributing editor to *Baseball Today* magazine and his byline has appeared in many hobby publications including *Sports Collectors Digest* and *Baseball Hobby News*. His writing and photography for coin collecting publications have won more than a half-dozen awards from the Numismatic Literary Guild.